Criminal Justice
Recent Scholarship

Edited by
Marilyn McShane and Frank P. Williams III

A Series from LFB Scholarly

The Effects of Race and Family Attachment on Self-Esteem, Self-Control, and Delinquency

Mahasin C. Owens-Sabir

LFB Scholarly Publishing LLC
New York 2007

Copyright © 2007 by LFB Scholarly Publishing LLC

Library of Congress Cataloging-in-Publication Data

Owens-Sabir, Mahasin Cecelia.
  The effects of race and family attachment on self-esteem, self-control, and delinquency / Mahasin C. Owens-Sabir.
      p. cm. -- (Criminal justice : recent scholatship)
  Includes bibliographical references and index.
  ISBN 978-1-59332-211-3 (alk. paper)
  1. Juvenile delinquency--United States. 2. Family--United States. 3. Race--United States. 4. Self esteem--United States. 5. Self-control--United States. I. Title.
  HV9104.O985 2007
  364.360973--dc22

2007009788

ISBN 9781593322113

Printed on acid-free 250-year-life paper.

Manufactured in the United States of America

Table of Contents

List of Tables and Figures

TABLE Page

Table of Contents   _ix_

TABLE   Page

FIGURE

Acknowledgments

I am most grateful for all of those who assisted me throughout the most challenging endeavor of my life. First and foremost I am most thankful for the wealth of knowledge and the assistance of Dr. Peter Wood, who patiently guided me through this process. Dr. Xiaohe Xu helped me relax and start to enjoy learning statistics. I appreciate his applied approach to teaching as well as his patience and understanding. Thanks to Dr. Robert Boyd for the time he committed to editing my work and helping me to understand that I don't have to rely on dichotomous thinking. I appreciate Dr. Matthew Lee, who helped me understand the value in the community approach and how sometimes helping the group can get more done much faster than just focusing on the individual.

Many individuals including professors, friends, and family have helped me as well as challenged my resolve; otherwise I would not be who I am today. I am grateful to all of them.

This book would not be a reality without the efforts and the assistance provided by Mr. Leo Balk of LFB Scholarly Publishing Co. Thank you.

CHAPTER 1

Introduction

What is the role of social bonding in the development of delinquency? What is the impact of self-control on delinquency, and is self-esteem significant in this relationship? These questions are central to this research, and the answers will help in understanding the factors that are crucial for the prevention of delinquency. The theories that provide the frameworks for this research are Hirschi's social bonding theory, Kaplan's general theory, and Gottfredson and Hirschi's self-control theory. Hirschi's social bonding theory explains why deviance is avoided. Kaplan's general theory offers explanatory factors that impact deviant responses. Gottfredson and Hirschi's self-control theory describes pre-existing characteristics of those who become involved in deviant behavior.

A central theoretical concern is the relationship between social bonding and self-control. A specific goal of this research is to examine the linkage between the two theories and their relationship to self-esteem. The approach used in this research is to examine social bonding and self-control on a continuum, which begins with the individual at an early age and progresses to adulthood; eventually impacting how the individual interacts in society. The general hypothesis is that social bonding at an early age with significant others, such as parents or guardians, has an impact on the development of self-control and, consequently, on involvement in delinquent activities.

The general theory of deviance is a comprehensive theory that includes elements of other theories, and it specifically examines the relationship between self-esteem and delinquency. Social bonding theory focuses on the importance of family and parenting as they relate

1

to delinquency, and self-control theory examines how individuals develop self-control. In this research, social bonding is defined as the closeness between the individual and others, primarily parents/guardians. Self-control is defined as the propensity to refrain from committing crimes or deviant acts. Delinquency refers to criminal acts committed by adolescents, and self-esteem describes the feelings individuals have about themselves.

This research examines the relative effects of social bonding, self-control and self-esteem on juvenile delinquency. Specifically, the aim is to investigate whether the proposed association between social bonding and delinquency is mediated – in part or in whole – by self-control and self-esteem. In addition, the associations are observed to see if they vary by race. Race is a key indicator of differences that may have significant sociological implications. Indices are used to measure self-esteem, social bonding and delinquency. Self-esteem and social bonding are measured by self-described feelings and situations, and delinquency is measured by a set of self-reported delinquent acts. The Grasmick et al. (1993) self-control scale is used. Race-specific analyses examine group differences in measures of self- and social-control and their impact on self-esteem and delinquency. Racial groups in this study are Native Americans, African Americans, and Whites.

The focus of this research is on youths, and the findings may be used to develop programs for prevention that are designed to decrease the number of youths participating in delinquent activities. A major shortcoming of the research in this area is the limited examination of social bonding, self-esteem, and self-control, as they relate to delinquency among nonwhite ethnic groups. Most of the literature on this subject examines delinquency among young, white males. This study, in contrast, includes both male and female Native Americans and African Americans. Since there is so little information on ethnic minorities in relation to the focus of this research, one of the objectives is to assist with filling that void; however, it is acknowledged at the onset that the limited available research made it more challenging to do so with confidence in the findings.

Many adolescents avoid becoming involved in delinquency while others from the same neighborhoods or environments engage in delinquent behavior. The primary motivation for this research is to search for answers to the question of why some youths become involved in delinquent behavior while others do not. The social bonding theory was chosen to guide this research specifically because of the significant role of the family in the prevention of delinquency.

Travis Hirschi's social bonding theory does not specify which institution has precedence when discussing attachment, which Hirschi (1969) describes as the most important element in bonding. This research adopts the premise that the institution of family, specifically parents/guardians, has the primary and foremost position in the early life of the child. Therefore, social bonding to the family, assuming the family is not criminogenic, is the foundation for the prevention of early delinquency that ultimately leads to criminal activity. Moreover, it is expected that social bonding to the family will be significant in the development of self-control. The study of self-esteem and delinquency covers a period of more than four decades. The self-esteem model of deviance hypothesizes a relationship between negative self-attitudes and delinquency. According to this model, low self-esteem, particularly self-derogation, is the motivation for participating in delinquent behavior as a means of restoring self-esteem (Kaplan, 1978; Rosenberg et al., 1989; Anderson, 1994). However, self-esteem is measured in the present but delinquency is measured by past actions. In this study, self-esteem is defined as "how one feels" about him/her self, and it will be used synonymously with "self-concept." Although violent and nonviolent crimes are examined in this research, the primary interest is delinquency because the goal is to use the information for prevention, which requires an understanding of initial entry into deviant behavior. A window of opportunity may exist for prevention of delinquency when children are younger, rather than waiting until later when the risk of involvement in delinquency is greater.

Increased self-control in the individual is the desired goal of advocates for the prevention of delinquency. The effects of self-control on delinquency are firmly established. According to Gottfredson and Hirschi (1990), all of the traits associated with low self-control often appear in the *absence* of nurturing, discipline, and training. This assumption separates self-control theory from most other theories of crime which usually perceive the offender to be "a product of positive forces, a creature of learning, particular pressures, or specific defect" (Gottfredson and Hirschi, 1990:95). Gottfredson and Hirschi lay the foundation for the importance of social bonding to the family, where nurturing, discipline and training first take place. Research presented here examines the relationship between self and social controls, self-esteem and delinquency. However, it should be noted that this research is largely exploratory primarily because the available research on self-control and social bonding as they relate to minorities is very limited. Consequently, the data are examined from several perspectives to ensure that as much information can be gathered from this effort as possible. In addition to the typical univariate and bivariate analyses, both logistic regression and OLS regression are utilized. Several of the variables (self-control, self-esteem and social bonding) are examined as both independent and dependent variables. Finally, some effort to explore theoretical integration is undertaken to see if a possible link exists between social bonding and self-control. Hopefully, the findings in this research will motivate further investigation of the topics examined here.

CHAPTER 2

Social Bonding, the General Theory of Deviance, and Self-Control

INTRODUCTION

Three theories of crime are used to examine delinquency in this research: social bonding theory, the general theory of deviance, and self-control theory. Social bonding theory is primary because it focuses on the early developmental years of children. The general theory of deviance addresses the issue of self-esteem. Self-control theory allows for an examination of behavior that leads to or prevents delinquency. Each of these theories is discussed in this chapter.

Social Bonding Theory

Social bonding theory is a social control theory that specifically addresses delinquency. It developed out of early efforts to understand external and internal methods of social control. Glueck and Glueck (1950) argued that sociocultural (especially family) forces influenced delinquent behavior. They concluded that the familial background of the delinquents they studied was "less adequate than that of the non-delinquents" (Glueck and Glueck, 1950:18). The homes of these youths were characterized by desertion, separation, divorce, or death of one or both parents, which made it difficult for bonding to take place during the formative years. Therefore, they were less likely to be exposed to the three minimum requirements for the development of self-control: monitoring behavior; recognition of deviant behavior; and punishment for engaging in deviant behavior.

Reiss (1950), one of the early pioneers of social bonding theory, believed delinquency resulted from a lack of personal and social controls. He described personal controls as "internal" and social controls as "external." Nye (1958) identified three forms of social control: direct, indirect and internal control. Nye believed indirect control was more effective in reducing delinquency than direct control because direct control relied upon the formal sanctioning of the legal system for enforcement. Indirect control is informal and is initiated by the family. Nye felt the family could be most instrumental in the prevention of delinquency if it were understood how crucial family involvement is during the formative years. Reckless (1961) also focused on internal and external controls; however, he described "pushes" and "pulls" during adolescence as having considerable power over who becomes delinquent. Adolescents are "pushed" toward delinquency when they come from families where conditions such as deprivation or poverty exist. If they become involved with peers who exert negative influences, they are "pulled" toward delinquency. The push and pull forces can be counteracted by informal outer containment, such as family and school or inner containment, such as a strong self-concept.

Hirschi's (1969) social bonding theory is central to criminology and is one of the most frequently tested theories in the discipline. Hirschi brought together elements from all previous control theories and developed empirical measures for each concept. He argues that delinquency is the result of weakened or broken bonds to society. The four primary components of Hirschi's theory are attachment, commitment, involvement and beliefs. According to Hirschi's findings, an individual is more likely to become delinquent when attachment to significant others is absent.   Commitment implies acceptance of conformity. This principle motivates the individual to consider his or her own interests and those of others in society and builds a desire to refrain from endangering them by committing criminal acts and deviant acts in general. Involvement requires participation in conventional activities (such as school, work, family), which reduces the time available to participate in crime. Beliefs refer to the acceptance of norms and laws and their moral validity.

Attachment is the cornerstone of Hirschi's social bonding theory. Hirschi (1969) emphasizes the significance of attachment when he declares that the essence of the internalization of norms lies in the attachment of the individual to others.   This analogy is important because it positions the concept of attachment in such a way that it can be measured independently of deviant behavior.

Hirschi proposes that delinquent acts are the result of weak or broken bonds to society. If the bonds to society are weakened, the individual is less sensitive to the concerns of others, and he or she cares less about violating the shared norms of society.   Thus, a person's beliefs about society are determined by the extent to which that person accepts the norms and values of society.   Therefore, if a person has strong beliefs about conformity, he or she will be less likely to violate society's norms (Hirschi, 1969; Akers, 2000). Hirschi further contends that a person is free to deviate when he or she does not care about the wishes, expectations or opinions of others in society, which results in alienation and interpersonal conflict.   Consequently, attachment is necessary for the internalization of norms, which leads to the development of conscience.

A low level of family connectedness is associated with adolescents seeking approval and support from peers.   Therefore, weak family bonding may directly influence peer association and deviant behavior. Alienation from family, or disruption in family dynamics, such as parent-child bonding, may lead to adolescent defiance and loss of family cohesiveness.

Self-Esteem and Kaplan's General Theory of Deviance

As early as 1967, Walter Reckless presented what was termed "pioneering research" on the self-concept as an insulator against delinquency in his containment theory (Reckless and Dinitz, 1967). Reckless and Dinitz argued that it was no longer feasible for sociologists and criminologists to focus on the impact of disorganized or disadvantaged neighborhoods, family tensions, gangs or illegitimate opportunities as explanations of deviant behavior.   The researchers recommended that sociologists work with psychologists and psychiatrists to search for "the self factors" which influence behavior. Once the "self factors" are identified, the next task is to discover how they can be controlled.

Differences in delinquent behavior among youths from the same neighborhood can be found in comparing self-concepts. Those youths who do not participate in delinquency are found to have "a good self-concept" which is believed to be a product of favorable socialization. Conversely, a poor self-concept is considered to be a product of unfavorable socialization (Reckless and Dinitz, 1967). Their hypotheses were supported in a study of sixth-grade students. The findings indicated that self-concept may be an important "self-factor" in determining the "drift" toward or away from delinquency and crime (Reckless and Dinitz, 1967:522).

Hirschi and Selvin (1967) described the relationship between delinquency and self-concept as follows:

> "In our quest to discover what insulates a boy against delinquency in a high delinquency area, we believe we have some tangible evidence that a good self concept, undoubtedly a product of favorable socialization, veers slum boys away from delinquency, while a poor self concept, a product of unfavorable socialization, gives the slum boy no resistance to deviancy, delinquent companions, or delinquent sub-culture" (p. 264).

According to Reckless's containment theory, a favorable self-concept is necessary to insulate the individual against deviance, and it must be accompanied by necessary social control factors that impede the expression of deviance (Reckless, 1961). Facets of control and containment theories are incorporated within the general theory. Moreover, if the individual receives gratification from the normative structure, he or she will experience positive self-feelings and develop positive ties to society, which precipitates seeking valued goals through legitimate means. However, the individual may have feelings of self-rejection if he or she experiences adverse outcomes from interacting within society, and those feelings may prevent the development of strong personal ties with the normative structure. These same individuals are less likely to see themselves as needing to conform to societal expectations. Therefore, alternative deviant means of self-enhancement might lead to deviant responses.

The General Theory of Deviance

Kaplan's general theory includes many facets of other theories of deviance, particularly those of strain, control, containment and labeling. Strain theory offers the view of deviant responses as "outcomes of the disjunctions between culturally prescribed (and personally internalized) goals and institutionalized means for achieving these goals" (Kaplan, 1982:193). According to control theories, if an individual experiences satisfaction in normal everyday socialization he or she is more likely to accept the norms or society, and less likely to adopt deviant behavior (Kaplan, 1982).

A controversial feature of the self-enhancement model is a potential curvilinear relationship between self-esteem and delinquency, whereby lower self-esteem can lead to delinquent behavior and, at some point, delinquent behavior can then lead to greater self-esteem. Wells and Rankin (1983) tested this hypothesis. Ultimately, Wells and Rankin determined the relationship between delinquency and self-concept to be problematic.

Causation was found to be in a different direction by McCarthy and Hoge (1984). They observed that as delinquent behavior increases, self-esteem decreases. No significant relationship was found for adolescents who initially had low self-esteem, but a greater negative effect of delinquency on subsequent self-esteem was found for adolescents who were initially high in self-esteem. According to the findings, adolescents view some delinquent behavior as "normative." Therefore, it does not have a negative effect on self-esteem, and it may in some cases enhance self-esteem. It appears that the seriousness of the offense influences the direction of the effect. Those offenses that were more serious had a greater negative effect on self-esteem.

The debate is ongoing in reference to the effects of self-esteem on delinquency. Wells (1989) contends that self-esteem does not directly affect delinquent behavior. He argues, "low self-esteem causes delinquent dispositions or motivations, which in turn cause delinquent behavior in conjunction with other social situational variables" (Wells, 1989:229). Wells maintains that the drive for self-enhancement is strong only when self-esteem decreases to a level where it creates a "tipping point." At this point anxiety is produced along with a motivational need to increase self-esteem. Therefore, enhancement motivation gets stronger as self-derogation intensifies. Wells' (1989) study using this model found that delinquent or deviant behavior may have an enhancing effect on self-esteem. However, the effect is more pronounced when applied to serious forms of delinquency (theft, vandalism, or fighting). Rosenberg et al. (1989) describe a similar relationship as "countervailing," in which a weak bivariate relationship is found because high self-esteem lowers delinquency and high delinquency may cause an increase in self-esteem.

Kaplan's general theory was tested in a study of 1,756 junior high school students. The researchers found that students were not motivated to conform if they felt that self-rejection was associated with the school environment, and they were inclined to deviate from "the normative expectations" of the school environment. The researchers found this to be true regardless "of the effects of race, sex, age, mother's educational level, and earlier academic failure" (Kaplan and Peck, 1994:3).

Self-Esteem and Race

According to Hughes and Hertel (1990) the issue of skin color affects every aspect of life chances for African Americans, in spite of the many social, political, and cultural changes that have taken place in the past century. Skin color impacts life for African Americans, and the impacts can be traced back to social differentiation by skin color during the antebellum period up to the present time. During this time some African Americans still believed that opportunities were fewer not only because of their race, but also because of the darkness or lightness of their skin color (Hughes and Hertel, 1990; Cross, 1991; Hill, 2000).

The interacting effect of race on findings about the relationship between self-esteem and delinquency was neglected by earlier studies. In fact, most of the studies were limited to white males. The present study is limited to personal identity measures, but Ross (1994) included group identity measures when he studied the effects of "race-esteem" and self-esteem on delinquency. Ross tested the proposition that high levels of self-esteem control delinquent behavior, and low levels of self-esteem contribute to delinquent behavior. He thought it was important to distinguish between different measures of self-esteem for individuals from different racial backgrounds. In other words, he suggests that persons in different racial groups may differ in their perception of self-esteem.

Ross (1994) observed a significant inverse correlation between race-esteem and delinquency for Whites. Both personal and group identity measures of self-esteem predicted delinquency for African Americans. African Americans were less likely to be delinquent when they were more confident of success (personal or self-esteem), and when they were proud to be a member of their race or ethnic group

(group or race-esteem). Ross's group or race-esteem is described by some researchers as "collective identities," which refer to an identification with the social group to which an individual belongs (Luhtanen and Crocker, 1992; Katz et al., 2002).

Owens (1994) also tested the interacting effect of race when he examined the relationship between positive self-worth and self-deprecation on adolescent problems. He found that African-American youths exhibited a stronger effect of teacher evaluations on self-worth. Poor grades had a powerful impact on self-deprecation for this group.

Self-Control Theory

According to Gottfredson and Hirschi, "people who lack self-control will tend to be impulsive, insensitive, physical rather than mental, risk-taking, short-sighted, and nonverbal, and they will tend, therefore, to engage in criminal and analogous acts" (Gottfredson and Hirschi, 1990:90). They argue that these traits are identifiable early in life. Gottfredson and Hirschi developed self-control theory as a general theory of crime, capable of explaining all criminal and "analogous behavior," regardless of race, geographic location or other demographics.

Individuals with high self-control have the capacity to defer gratification, and this effectively reduces the probability of crime throughout the life course. Contrary to high self-control, low self-control requires the immediate gratification of desires or as Gottfredson and Hirschi (1990) describe it, a "here and now" orientation. Criminal acts satisfy these immediate desires; "they provide money without work, sex without courtship, and revenge without court delays" (Gottfredson and Hirschi, 1990:333). The authors also argue that pleasure is not necessarily the major benefit derived from crime. Physical abuse may be generated by such stimuli as irritation caused by a crying child or the taunting of a stranger in a bar. Those with low self-control usually have very little tolerance for frustration and limited ability to respond to conflict appropriately.

Individuals with low self-control do not calculate the long-term consequences of an act. Gottfredson and Hirschi (1990) maintain that an individual who does not calculate the consequences of his or her behavior is also impulsive or shortsighted, and that the major cause of low self-control is the absence of nurturing and discipline.

Gottfredson and Hirschi argue that socialization is primary to the development of self-control. Incomplete or ineffective socialization, specifically during the course of child rearing, is a key reason for low self-control. In addition, attachment to parents affects the level of self-control developed by children. Close supervision is a result of strong attachment between parents and children, and discipline is expected when norms are violated. Disapproval of deviant acts by parents is one of the most effective informal negative sanctions, and it decreases the likelihood that children will participate in delinquency or commit crimes as adults (Gottfredson and Hirschi, 1990). Therefore, Gottfredson and Hirschi (1990) recommend three minimum conditions necessary for adequate parental supervision: (1) monitor the child's behavior, (2) recognize deviant behavior when it occurs, and (3) punish such behavior.

Testing self-control theory prompted considerable debate among researchers relating to tautology. The discussions centered on Gottfredson and Hirschi's failure to differentiate between self-control and the propensity toward criminal behavior. This was especially significant since self-control is hypothesized to be the cause of the propensity toward criminal behavior. Consequently, the labels, "low self-control" and "high self-control," were used by Gottfredson and Hirschi to describe the differential propensity to commit or refrain from crime. Akers (2000) contends that they do not operationalize the measures of low self-control to be different from the tendency to commit crime that low self-control is suppose to explain. Therefore, the measures of criminal propensity, which is the dependent variable, are the same as the measures of self-control, the independent variable.

Some researchers have tried indirect measures of self-control, such as whether change in delinquent activities is caused by changing characteristics in the individual or the stability or change in the individual's environment (Benson and Moore, 1992; Nagin and Farrington, 1992). Mixed findings resulted from their research, showing both stability and change.

Despite this issue, Harold Grasmick and associates (1993) developed a scale of items designed to measure different dimensions of self-control described by Gottfredson and Hirschi. Research (Pratt and Cullen, 2000) using the scale designed by Grasmick et al. (1993) shows support for the inverse relationship between self-control and crime. Grasmick et al. (1993) found low self-control to be related to general law violations. Wood et al. (1993) report a relationship between low self-control and self-reported delinquency and crime. Arneklev et al. (1993) and Wood et al. (1993) also concluded that a relationship existed between low self-control and risk-taking behavior. Low socioeconomic status and weak social bonds are examples of low self-control that are related to negative life outcomes (Evans et al., 1997).

Self-Control and the Family

Ineffective parenting that lacks nurturing and discipline is believed to be the major cause of low self-control. If the person who cares for the child implements the three crucial requirements mentioned above, the child will be watched, informed when behaving inappropriately, and taught the appropriate behavior. Furthermore, there will be unpleasant consequences for additional inappropriate behavior. The results, according to Gottfredson and Hirschi (1990), will be a child more capable of delaying gratification, more sensitive of others, and more willing to respect boundaries. Deviance and violence will not be seen as options for satisfying wants and needs. It is absolutely necessary that preliminary specifications are in place, such as caring, time, and energy to monitor the child, recognizing inappropriate behavior, and punishing such behavior (Glueck and Glueck, 1950; West and Farrington, 1977). Failure to accomplish the above is defined as incomplete socialization. Adequate socialization requires that parents or guardians devote time to the proper behavior training of children, which takes into consideration the rights and feeling of others. Consideration of these rights and feelings serves as a constraint on the child's behavior if adequate socialization has taken place (Gottfredson and Hirschi, 1990). A study by Patterson et al. (1989) also found a relationship between a lack of parental supervision and participation in delinquent and violent behavior. They concluded that it is important for parents to be involved with their children whether monitoring, recognizing deviant behavior or resorting to effective and consistent discipline. These findings apply across ethnic and racial categories (Patterson et al., 1989).

Gottfredson and Hirschi contend that "all else being equal" one parent is sufficient and "proper training can be accomplished outside the confines of the two-parent home" (Gottfredson and Hirschi, 1990:104). However, they acknowledge that "all else is rarely equal," and therefore, it is quite challenging for a single parent to effectively monitor and discipline a child in the absence of psychological and social support, but it is possible. In fact, according to the authors, it is not even necessary for the adult training the child to be the guardian, as long as effective supervision occurs.

Social institutions such as schools contribute to socialization, but the family is believed to be the most important in the development of self-control. Gottfredson and Hirschi argue that peers are relatively unimportant in this development as it relates to involvement in delinquency. Insufficient socialization may occur in some instances, such as when parents lack self-control or when they are criminals. Other institutions, especially the school, are then expected to take on the responsibility for properly socializing children. Teachers are in a key position to sufficiently monitor behavior, recognize deviance, and discipline children, thus making the school a possible effective socializing agency. However, limited success has been realized by schools, primarily because of a lack of cooperation and support from parents. This implies a need for prerequisite social bonding to family. Gottfredson and Hirschi identify areas of influence on delinquency that schools can utilize. They stress that schools should still strive to have a positive effect on children, even if it is without parental support. A major predictor of crime in relationship to school is whether the child likes school or not. Glueck and Glueck (1950:144) noted that delinquents do not like school. In addition, school performance is also a strong predictor of delinquency and criminal activity.

Self-Control and Age

According to Gottfredson and Hirschi, the self-control acquired early in childhood remains relatively stable throughout life. They argue that low self-control may change over time, but the trait does not diminish with maturity or increased age. The general theory thesis is that the age effect is invariant across social and cultural conditions. The situational or life-course explanation for the decrease in crime with age attributes the decline to a change in an individual's source of satisfaction. However, according to Gottfredson and Hirschi (1990), this hypothesis is not supported by data. They contend that there is no drastic shuffling of the criminal population based on situational events. They further argue that the decline in crime that comes with age is not attributed to anything other than the maturation of the individual. Gottfredson and Hirschi (1990) make a clear distinction between crime and self-control, arguing that crime everywhere declines with age, while differences in "crime tendency" across individuals remain stable over the life course.

Self-Control and Gender

A consistent pattern has been established, primarily through the use of self-reported data, supporting the relationship between gender and crime. Male participation in serious crime is documented to exceed that of females, at any given age, regardless of the type of crime (Blumstein et al. 1986). Gender differences for all types of crimes begin early in life and they persist throughout the life course. According to Gottfredson and Hirschi (1990), gender differences in crime offenses imply a substantial self-control difference between the sexes.

    An ongoing debate exists on whether the gender differences in crime can be explained by differences in the types of crimes rather than criminality. For example, obvious gender differences exist if crimes such as rape and prostitution are examined.   There is also more approval of deviant behavior for males compared to females. Consequently, gender disparity in committing crimes may be explained primarily by differences in opportunity to commit crimes. Gottfredson and Hirschi (1990) further explain the gender differential by the presence or absence of direct parental supervision and the tighter control on girls. They conclude that lack of attachment to parents is related to delinquency for both boys and girls.

Self-Control and Race

As with age and gender, there is substantial agreement that stable differences exist in delinquency and crime rates across race and ethnic groups. Racial variations in crime most often focus on "the American black-white rate difference" and consequently explain racial and ethnic differences in crime by use of a "subculture of violence" argument (Gottfredson and Hirschi, 1990: 151). According to the subculture of violence thesis, deprivation leads to the development of values and a lifestyle that condones interpersonal violence (Wolfgang and Ferracuti, 1967). Another explanation for racial differences in crime is offered by "strain" theories. Strain theories focus on the outcomes of relative poverty among racial groups (Merton, 1938; Cloward and Ohlin, 1960; Blau and Blau, 1982). According to these theories, poverty or deprivation and perception of injustices among ethnic minorities produce strain, which then leads to crime. The focus is usually on relative rather than absolute poverty, specifically as it relates to a comparison between African Americans and Whites.

The use of income inequality by strain theorists as an explanation of racial differences in crime produced what is termed the "inequality thesis." The inequality thesis has been firmly denounced by some researchers on the basis that it lacks supporting evidence (Gottfredson and Hirschi, 1990; Sampson, 1985; Golden and Messner, 1987). Cultural models, such as the subculture of violence, are inadequate according to Gottfredson and Hirschi (1990), because they are too general. Social scientists have not been successful at assigning specific group differences in attitudes and values that can be used to predict crime. Furthermore, Gottfredson and Hirschi argue that empirical evidence does not support the assumptions. Likewise, they do not support strain theories because according to them the commission of criminal acts is "governed by the proximity, ease, and convenience of their rewards, rather than by compelling social or psychological purposes" as proposed by strain theorists (Gottfredson and Hirschi, 1990:152). They make the point that no social group starts out with the intention of purposefully reducing self-control of its member. Low self-control diminishes and undermines harmonious group relations and jeopardizes the accomplishment of group goals. This, according to Gottfredson and Hirschi, negates the assumption that crime is "a product of socialization, culture, or positive learning of any sort" (Gottfredson and Hirschi, 1990:339).

Gottfredson and Hirschi (1990) believe that there are differences among racial and ethnic groups in the levels of direct supervision, comparable to the gender differences. But they argue that differences in self-control probably outweigh supervision differences as an explanation for racial variations. Gottfredson and Hirschi advocate abandoning the theory that racial or ethnic differences in crime can be explained by culture or strain and instead focus on differences in child-rearing practices.

Social Bonding and Self-Control Theory

Hirschi did not claim self-control as part of his social bonding theory, and the self-control idea was originally subsumed under the concept of attachment. Gottfredson and Hirschi give no explanation in reference to why self-control became central to the control of deviant behavior. Akers (2000) speculates that it may be assumed that all four of the elements of social bonding are now subsumed under the concept of self-control. Likewise, Gottfredson and Hirschi's self-control theory makes no mention of the four elements of Hirschi's social bonding theory (Akers, 2000).

Gottfredson and Hirschi indicate no link between self-control and social bonding, although there are some indicators of this link in their description of self-control, particularly when describing the process of socialization and its dependence on attachment. Bonding to significant others is a necessary step in the process of developing self-control. Akers concludes that "self-control is the key variable, and other social bonds affect crime only indirectly through their effects on self-control" (Akers, 2000:111). Akers proposes linking the two to create a comprehensive perspective that will fill some of the gaps left by social bonding. He maintains that self-control can be viewed as relating to social bonding because social bonding is a prerequisite for the development of self-control (Akers, 2000).

Theory integration has been considered as a remedy for resolving differing conceptual approaches and creating greater predictive power by combining theories (Tittle, 2000). Recent research has focused on integrating social bonding and self-control theories into one explanatory model (Longshore et al., 2004). The rationale is that self-control impacts serious deviance at a distance because it develops over a span of years, therefore implying a causal process involving more immediate factors. One of the possible immediate or proximal factors is social bonding. Longshore et al. (2004) examine this proposition in a longitudinal study in which four aspects of social bonding (attachment, involvement, religious commitment, and moral belief) were studied. Low self-control, social bonds, and deviant peer association as predictors of drug use were observed over a six-month period. Self-control was found to be strongly and inversely related to all four measures of social bonding. The link examined in this study is a one-way model from low self-control to social bonds. However, the researchers acknowledge that "the causal processes may be more dynamic," whereby weak social ties early in life may undermine the development of adequate self-control (Longshore et al., 2004: 558). This research utilizes this causal process and applies it to a continuum.

Delinquency

The primary dependent variable in this study is delinquency. Delinquency among Whites, African Americans and Native Americans, is examined in this study. This section highlights delinquency statistics in general, and presents specific data for African Americans and Native Americans.

In 2002 U.S. courts with juvenile jurisdiction handled an estimated 2.3 million cases in which the juvenile was charged with a delinquency offense. Juvenile courts handled about one million individual juveniles charged with delinquency offenses in 1992. Juveniles accounted for 17 percent of all arrests and 15 percent of all violent crime arrests in 2002. A substantial growth in juvenile violent crime arrests began in the late 1980s and peaked in 1994. Since that time for eight consecutive years up to 2002, the rate of juvenile arrests for Violent Crime Index offenses has declined. However, juvenile crime remains a problem. Of the estimated 2.3 million arrests 92,160 were for violent offenses in 2002. In addition, arrest trends show females make up an increasing proportion of juvenile arrests. Minorities still account for a disproportionate percentage of juvenile arrests; however, there has been a decrease in the disparity in violent crime arrest rates for blacks and whites between 1980 and 2002 (Snyder, 2004).

In 2002 there were approximately 61,610 juvenile arrests for aggravated assault. Females made up 24 percent of juvenile arrests for aggravated assault and 32 percent of other forms of assault (i.e., simple assaults and intimidations). In addition, three out of every five (60%) juveniles arrested for running away from home were female. Juveniles committed 14 percent of robberies, 12 percent of aggravated assaults, and 20 percent of property crime offenses committed in 2002. The juvenile arrest rate for robbery declined between 1995 and 2002 to its lowest level since 1980, and though robbery also declined, it did not erase the increase that began in the mid-1980s. The juvenile arrest rate for aggravated assault was still 27 percent above the 1980 level in 2002 (Snyder, 2004). Confidential surveys reveal that approximately 15 percent of high school seniors committed an act of serious violence between 1993 and 1998. The number of violent acts by high school seniors has increased nearly 50 percent over the past two decades. Gang activity also increased between 1994 and 1999. After 1999 the proportion of schools in which gangs were present began to decline. However the number of youths involved in gangs has remained near the peak levels of 1996 (U.S. Department of Education Surgeon General's Report, 2001).

Although homicide is not the best measure of youth violence, it does offer a glimpse into the seriousness of the overall problem when 1,400 adolescents commit the offense in one year (U.S. Department of Education Surgeon General's Report, 2001). Homicide was the second leading cause of death among all youth aged 15-24 (20.3 per 100,000) in 2001, and was the leading cause of death among black youth aged 15-24 (74.4 per 100,000) in 2001. There is adequate evidence of the need for urgency in preventing a resurgence of the violence epidemic that swept the United States during the decade between 1983 and 1993. The Surgeon General warns us that the sizable number of youths still involved in violence only need to begin carrying and using weapons as they did a decade ago, and history will repeat itself.

The number of juvenile delinquents coming before juvenile courts has added an additional challenge for the system. Juvenile courts handled 180,000 juvenile offenders younger than 13 years of age in 1997. Juvenile delinquents younger than 13 years of age committed one in three arson offenses, one in five sex offenses, and one in 12 violent crime offenses. This is particularly significant because youth who enter the juvenile court system prior to age 13 are far more likely to become chronic juvenile offenders than those youth who enter the system at an older age. Child delinquents are two to three times more likely to become serious, violent, and chronic offenders than are adolescents whose delinquent behavior begins in their teens. High profile media cases of violence committed by children age 12 or younger also draw attention to the potential for juvenile delinquents to inflict deadly harm. Consequently, juvenile delinquents represent a significant concern for both society and the juvenile justice system (Office of Juvenile Justice Delinquency Prevention, 2003). The arrest rate of child delinquents increased by 45 percent between 1988 and 1997 (paralleling the increase in violence for all juveniles) and drug abuse violations increased by 156 percent (Snyder, 2001).

Research shows that not all disruptive children will become child delinquents, and not all child delinquents will become serious, violent, or chronic juvenile offenders. However, most violent and chronic juvenile offenders have a history of problem behavior that dates back to the childhood years. Antisocial careers of male juvenile offenders start, on average, at age seven, much earlier than the average age of first court contact for Crime Index offenses, which is age 14.5 (Office of Juvenile Justice Delinquency Prevention, 2003).

The racial breakdown of juvenile court referrals changed during the 10-year period between 1988 and 1997. During this period, child delinquent court cases increased by 41 percent for nonwhite youth and 28 percent for white youth. In addition, a greater proportion of the 1997 nonwhite cases (45 percent nonwhite cases versus 37 percent white cases) were placed on the court docket for an adjudicatory hearing (Snyder, 2001).

African Americans

African American youth are over represented in the juvenile justice system. They make up only 15 percent of the juvenile population but they account for 26 percent of the juveniles who are arrested. This is compared to White youth, who make up 79 percent of the juvenile population and are 71 percent of the juveniles arrested.   African American youth account for 42 percent of arrest for violent crime compared to 55 percent for White youth. The robbery arrest rate for African Americans is 54 percent compared to 43 percent for Whites. Court referral rates reflect an equal level of racial disparity (Office of Juvenile Justice Delinquency Prevention, 2002).

A greater proportion of person and drug offenses cases were processed in courts for black juveniles than for other juveniles. Property cases dominated the caseloads of all racial groups except for black juveniles. Among blacks, less than half of the cases handled were for property offenses, and more than 60 percent of property cases were for Whites and juveniles of other races. The person offense arrest rate for black juveniles in 1992 was four times the white rate, and for drug law violations it was about five times the rate for whites (Office of Juvenile Justice Delinquency Prevention, 2003).

Although juvenile involvement in crime has been generally consistent over the past several decades, the racial gap has widened, specifically for homicides by juveniles.   African American youth constitute the majority of the increase between 1986 and 1994, but they also are responsible for the majority of the decline since that period of time (Hawkins et al., 2000).

Sampson and Laud (1993) found that underclass poverty and racial inequality are related to an increase in juvenile justice processing of minorities.   According to them the rates of out-of-home placement (the most intrusive intervention possible) for African Americans were particularly striking.   They contend that the pattern is consistent with the idea that black males are a threat and should be subjected to increased formal social control.   Bishop and Frazier (1996) drew similar conclusions from their research.   Their findings indicated clear disadvantages for nonwhites at various stages of delinquency case processing, which they believe represents a consistent pattern of unequal treatment.

Native Americans

Native American youth must deal with the limitations experienced by other disadvantaged youths, as well as a negative historical legacy and negative stereotyping.   They must also struggle with the discrepancies between cultural myth and social reality (Lin, 1987).   As members of a disadvantaged racial minority group, Lin argues that Native Americans, specifically females, fall victim to the problems associated with poverty, prejudice and discrimination.   In addition to high crime rates, domestic violence, child abuse and neglect, Native Americans also suffer alcohol abuse and gang involvement. These factors expose Native American youth to multiple risk factors for delinquency (Office of Juvenile Justice Delinquency Prevention, 2003).

According to the Office of Juvenile Justice Delinquency Prevention Annual Report (2002) Native Americans have an arrest rate that is three times that of African Americans and ten times the White arrest rate.   Native Americans have a violent crime rate that is twice the national rate. The number of Native Americans in the Federal Bureau of Prisons' custody has increased 50 percent since 1994, and Native Americans make up more than 70 percent of the approximately 270 youth in the Bureau's custody on any given day. The violent crime rate for Native Americans in 1998 was nearly 20 percent above the average rate of the 1980s (Office of Juvenile Justice Delinquency

Prevention Annual Report, 2002). Native American youth constitute more than two percent of the youth arrested for offenses such as larceny-theft and liquor law violations even though they represent only one percent of the population. In four states (South Dakota, Alaska, North Dakota, and Montana), Native American youth make up 29 to 42 percent of youth in confinement. Alcohol related deaths are 17 times higher than the national average for Native American youth ages 15-24. The use of alcohol, cigarettes, and marijuana has been reported to be disproportionately higher among Native American youth (Beauvais, 1992). The reported lifetime and 30-day marijuana use rates for Native Americans were 77 percent and 33 percent, respectively, compared to rates of 38 percent and 13 percent for white adolescents (Beauvais, 1992).

Compared to non-Indian youth, Native American youth show very high rates of drug use. About 20 percent of Native American adolescents continue to be heavily involved with drugs even though overall drug use is decreasing, and this has been the trend since 1980 (Beauvais, 1992). Marijuana use is particularly high among Native American youth, and a significant number of Native American students have tried drugs by the 7th grade, regardless of gender (Beauvais et al., 1989; Beauvais, 1992). Tobacco use, including smokeless tobacco use, is also high among Native American youth compared to the overall U.S. population (Spangler, 1997). Spangler's study of Native American women found 20.6 percent to be current smokeless tobacco users, and 23.7 percent were current smokers. According to Spangler, smokeless tobacco use correlates with lower education. Smoking is correlated with age, alcohol use, separation or divorce and lack of friends.

Statement of Hypotheses

This study will test whether the predicted relationships between social bonding, self-esteem, self-control and delinquency are in accord with the assumptions of social bonding and self-control theories. Therefore, variables that measure self-control, self-esteem and social bonding theories are utilized in this study. Particular attention is devoted to the impact of parenting as conceptualized by Gottfredson and Hirschi (1990); the variables of monitoring, recognition and punishing make up the core of parental supervision and are at the very foundation of social bonding. The assumption is that if this foundation is weak, all other aspects of social bonding will be minimized. In addition, it is proposed that a significant positive relationship exists between the variables that make up social bonding and self-esteem. Consequently, it is hypothesized that high scores on social bonding will result in high scores on self-esteem. Likewise, high scores on social bonding are believed to indicate high scores on self-control. In the final analysis, each of the hypothesized relationships will be examined for race differences. Figure 1 depicts the hypothesized relationships. The hypothesized relationships are as follows:

H_1: Social bonding is negatively related to delinquency.

H_2: Social bonding is positively related to self-control.

H_3: Social bonding is positively related to self-esteem.

H_4: The effect of social bonding on delinquency is mediated by self-esteem.

H_5: Self-control is negatively related to delinquency.

H_6: The impact of social bonding on delinquency is mediated by self-control.

H_7: Self-control is positively related to self-esteem.

H_8: Net of other predictors, self-esteem has a negative impact on delinquency.

H_9: The relative impacts of social bonding, self-control and self-esteem on delinquency will vary by race.

H_{10}: The relative impacts of social bonding, self-control, and delinquency on self-esteem will vary by race.

H_{11}: Net of other predictors, delinquency has a positive impact on self-esteem.

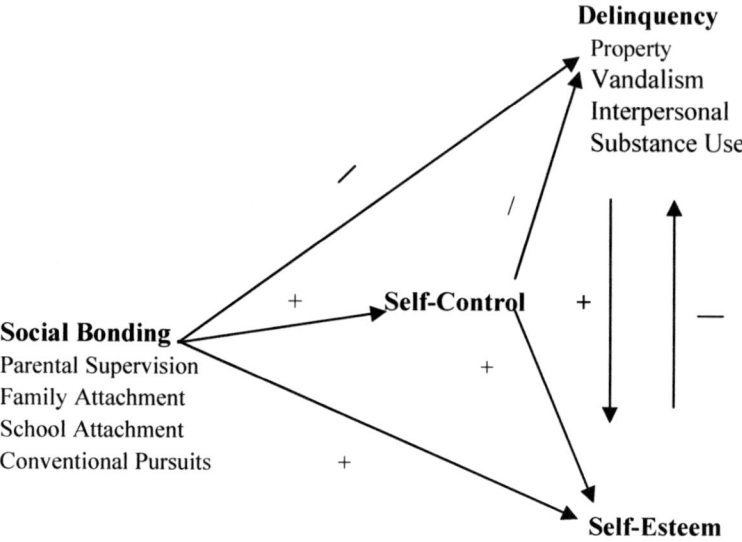

Figure 1: Diagram of Hypothesized Relationships

CHAPTER 3

The Data Set and Variables

INTRODUCTION

The data for this study are from a secondary data set, consisting of respondents in the *High School Delinquency Survey, 1991-1994*, collected by the Department of Sociology, Center for the Study of Crime, Delinquency, and Social Control, at the University of Oklahoma. The respondents are a mix of urban and rural public high school students living in Oklahoma. Six school districts with grades 9-12 are represented. The school districts are from each region of the state (central, northeast, southeast, northwest, and southwest). The total number of respondents used in this study is 1724. The racial composition is as follows: White, 1122, African American, 220 and Native American Indian, 382. The questionnaire was administered to all students in attendance who volunteered to participate in the study, and who had obtained written permission from their parents. This included approximately 43 percent of the total school enrollment in the six schools. Research staff and school officials administered the questionnaire.

The data are non-representative because a random sample was not used. Some limitations are also inherent in the use of self-reported data. The nature of self-reported data increases the likelihood that respondents will alter their responses to enhance how they present themselves. Conversely, respondents may paint a very negative picture of themselves for any number of reasons including amusement or to influence what will happen to them as a result of their answers. Respondents may also choose certain answers because they are more socially acceptable. All of the described represent the disadvantages inherent in self-reported data that may create questions about validity or reliability, but the advantages continue to influence the use of self-reported data. The advantages of using self-reported data include the ease of administering to large samples, the data are easy to quantify and analyze, and self-reports allow respondents the choice of skipping items that they do not want to answer (Richter, 2001).

The inclusion of minorities in this study addresses one of the criticisms of prior research on delinquency. The fact that Native Americans, a population that has been understudied, are over represented in this study justifies the research. However, the number of African Americans in this study is not representative of the population. These facts plus the disadvantages of self-reported data make it necessary to emphasize the exploratory nature of this research and remind the reader that the findings should not be generalized to the overall population.

The Dependent Variables

Two dependent variables are used, delinquency and self-esteem. The primary dependent variable is delinquency. Four categories of delinquency will be examined – property offenses, interpersonal offenses, vandalism, and substance/drug use. The delinquency variables used in this study are measures of self-reported past delinquency. A description of each delinquency measure is listed below.

Property Delinquency

A single composite measure was created with five items that produced an eigenvalue of 2.23 and factor loadings ranging from .52 - .79 (Cronbach's alpha = .61). The property scale - About how many times this past year have you: Taken a car without permission for a joyride; Taken something from a car (tapedeck, wallet, purse, hubcaps, mirrors, etc.) without permission; Taken/Stolen something from someone else worth more than $5; Taken/Stolen something from someone else worth less than $50; and Taken something from a store without paying for it (shoplifted).

Vandalism Delinquency

A single composite measure was created with five items that produced an eigenvalue of 2.94 and factor loadings ranging from .55 - .85 (Cronbach's alpha = .80). The vandalism scale - About how many times this past year have you: Damaged (scratched, dented, painted, vandalized, etc.) a car on purpose; Gone into or broken into a house or building when you weren't supposed to be there; Set fire to someone else's stuff/property; Damaged school property on purpose; and Damaged property at work on purpose.

Interpersonal Delinquency

A single composite measure was created with five items that produced an eigenvalue of 2.78 and factor loadings ranging from .65 - .84 (Cronbach's alpha = .76). The interpersonal scale - About how many times this past year have you: Gotten into a serious fight at work or school; Used a gun or knife or some other thing (like a club) to get something from a person; Hurt someone badly enough to need bandages or a doctor; Hit an instructor or supervisor; and Taken part in a fight where a group of your friends were against another group.

Substance/Drug Use Delinquency

The survey responses for the substance/drug use items include "everyday/all the time/all 4 weeks" (00-28), sometimes/often/several/ once in a while" (98), and "don't know/no answer/not applicable" (99). A single composite measure was created with five items, with an eigenvalue of 3.06 and factor loadings ranging from .57-.90 (Cronbach's alpha = .74). The substance/drug use scale - About how many days in the past four weeks did you: Smoke cigarettes or chew tobacco; Drink beer, wine, or liquor; Get drunk on beer, wine, or liquor; Smoke marijuana, pot, hash; and Use drugs like cocaine, crack, speed, downers, heroin, LSD, or angel dust (PCP).

Self-Esteem

Self-esteem is used primarily as a predictor in this research; however, it is also analyzed as a dependent variable to examined a possible positive relationship, shown in Figure 1, between delinquency and self-esteem.

It is measured by an index of seven survey items. Items were recoded to indicate that high scores on the scale reflect greater self-esteem. Survey item responses were recoded to reflect 1 = strongly disagree to 4= strongly agree. A single composite measure was created with the seven items (Cronbach's alpha = .73). The self-esteem scale is as follows: I take a positive attitude toward myself; I am reliable; I feel I do not have much to be proud of; I am trustworthy; On the whole, I am satisfied with myself; When I do a job, I do it well; and I wish I could have more respect for myself.

The Independent Variables

The primary independent variables represent concepts borrowed from social bonding and self-control theories. Self-esteem is examined as both a dependent variable and an independent variable. When predicting delinquency, self-esteem is an independent variable, and when predicting self-esteem, delinquency is an independent variable. Therefore, the same descriptive information on self-esteem as a dependent variable applies to its use as an independent variable.

Social Bonding

Social bonding is represented by the use of scales to measure parental supervision, family attachment, school attachment and involvement in conventional pursuits. Other researchers (Cochran et al., 1998; Loeber and Stouthamer-Loeber, 1986) have used the parental supervision scale Survey item responses were recoded to reflect 4 = strongly agree to 1= strongly disagree. High scores indicate a high degree of parental supervision. A single composite measure was created with three items, with an eigenvalue of 1.75 and factor loadings ranging from .72 - .82 (Cronbach's alpha = .64). The parental supervision scale is as follows: Generally, when I was younger my parents/guardians: Kept a pretty close eye on me (monitored behavior); Recognized when I had done something wrong (recognized deviant behavior); and punished me when they knew I had done something wrong (punished for deviant behavior). The survey responses for family attachment are true = 0 and false = 1. A higher number reflects more family attachment. The scale consists of six items. The items are a subset of two scales from the California Personality Inventory (CPI). They are recoded as indicated in the CPI manual so that higher values indicate higher levels of attachment. Some items are recoded to indicate that "1" is more attachment (Cronbach's alpha = .72). Family attachment is measured by an index consisting of the following survey items: I have very few quarrels with members of my family; My home life was always happy; I have often gone against my parents' wishes; The members of my family were always very close to each other; My parents never really understood me; and I sometimes wanted to run away from home.

A six-item scale was used to measure school attachment. The first two items consist of the choices: strongly agree, agree somewhat, disagree somewhat, and strongly disagree. Item three has the following answer choices: I like school very much, I like school quite a bit, I like school some, I don't like school very much, and I don't like school at all. Item four has answer choices on a scale of 1-5 that relate to frequency (almost always, often, sometimes, seldom and never). Item five reflects degree of excitement (very exciting and stimulating, quite interesting, fairly interesting, slightly dull and very dull). Item six refers to the importance of learning with the following choices: very important, quite important, fairly important, slightly important and not at all. All items were recoded so that high scores on the scale reflect greater school attachment. A single composite measure was created consisting of the six items with an eigenvalue of 3.04 (Cronbach's alpha = .80). The following survey items are used to measure school attachment: Going to school has been an enjoyable experience for me; Doing well in school is important for getting a good job; Some people like school very much. Others don't. How do you feel about going to school? How often do you feel the schoolwork you are assigned is meaningful and important? How interesting are most of your courses to you? How important do you think the things you are learning in school are going to be for your later life?

Items in the scale for involvement in conventional pursuits were recoded for high scores to equal to greater involvement in conventional pursuits (Cronbach's alpha = .56). The scale -- About how many days in the past four weeks did you do each of the following: Participated in community affairs or volunteer work; Played a musical instrument or sing; Actively participated in sports; athletics, or exercising; Did art or craft work.; Did creative writing; Worked around the house, yard, garden, car, etc.; Read books, magazines, or newspapers; or Went shopping or window-shopping?

Self-Control

The standard self-control scale developed by Grasmick et al. (1993) and used by other researchers (Arneklev et al., 1993; Longshore et al., 1996; Pratt and Cullen, 2000) is used in this study. The twenty-four-item scale consists of six categories of low self-control, which include risk seeking, self-centeredness, simple task preference, impulsiveness, temper, and preference for physical activities over mental activities. Each category is measured by the use of four survey items for a total of twenty-four items on the scale (see Appendix A). The responses range from 1= strongly agree to 4= strongly disagree. Items were recoded for high scores to indicate more self-control (Cronbach's alpha = .88).

The scale tested by Grasmick et al. (1993) is based on Gottfredson and Hirschi's formulation of the theory of self-control (Pratt and Cullen, 2000). The scale was tested by Grasmick et al. on an Oklahoma City sample of 395 adults, age 18 years or older, who were drawn from the general population. The researchers used exploratory factor analysis and concluded that there was strong evidence that combining items into subgroups produced applicable "multidimensionality" (Grasmick et al., 1993:17). The decision was made to omit one item and use a 23-items scale based on Cronbach's alpha results on a one-factor solution. Wood, Pfefferbaum, and Arneklev (1993) decided to retain all 24 items. They used both individual subscales and the self-control scale to produce findings that led them to conclude that the efficiency of the total scale and the subscales depended on the type of risky behavior tested. They also concluded that when self-control measures are used as a composite they should be studied using a multidimensional approach (Wood et al., 1993). The 24-item scale was used in this study.

Vazsonyi et al. (2001) examined the psychometric properties of the scale by Grasmick et al. on a large sample (N = 8,417). The sample is representative of adolescents in Hungary, the Netherlands, Switzerland

and the United States. The findings indicate: (1) the self-control measure is multidimensional; (2) the self-control measure is tenable for males, females, and ages 15-19; (3) deviance can be reliably measured in different countries; (4) self-control accounts for 10 to 16 percent of the total variance explained in different types of deviance and for 20 percent in total deviance; and (5) developmental processes involving self-control and deviance are largely invariant by national context (p. 91).

Control Variables

Control variables are as follows: average grade measured by grade point average; race (Native American, African American, and White); age based on year of birth; and gender (male or female). Specific emphasis will be placed on how social bonding, self-esteem and self-control vary by race. It can be assumed that there will be differences determined by each group's status in society, which affects the associations examined in this study. Race is also a key variable when studying self-esteem especially when comparing the dominant group (whites) with minorities (Native Americans and African Americans). A limitation of prior studies is the failure to use race-specific analyses.

Data Analyses

Univariate analysis is used to examine three major characteristics of the variables: distribution, central tendency, and dispersion. Demographic data are presented for each racial group in this study (Native American, African American, and White). The central tendency of the distributions is described by the mean and median. The spread of the values is measured by the standard deviation.

Bivariate associations are examined for evidence of relationships among the variables. Three characteristics are evaluated: (1) the existence of association, (2) the strength of the association, and (3) the direction or pattern of the association. Pearson's r is used to measure the correlations among the variables. T-tests are used to determine if there are statistically significant differences between the mean scores for the groups.

Multivariate analyses are used to examine the effects of the multiple predictor variables and their simultaneous relationship with the dependent variables. Multivariate analyses will allow for the documentation of collective effects and the examination of potentially spurious associations by using control variables. The multivariate analyses used in this study include both logistic regression and Ordinary Least Squares (OLS) regression. Logistic regression is used to determine the probability of something happening, and OLS will reveal the incidence, or the extent of occurrence. The sample size varies across the dependent variables. The number of observations within the same dependent variable is held constant by the use of listwise deletion, which is necessary for model comparisons. Logistic regression is used in this study to adjust for the disproportionate number of zeroes in the responses. Logistic regression creates estimates for the likelihood that an event will occur, given a set of conditions. The four measures of delinquency – interpersonal, property, vandalism and substance/drug use were recoded as 0/1 to indicate if the condition is or is not present (where 0 = no delinquency and 1 = some delinquency). Linear regression is one of the most powerful approaches to performing multivariate analyses. OLS regression is used to examine whether the increase in the predictor variables is associated with a consistent and constant increase or decrease in the amount of self-reported delinquency and self-esteem. In addition, social bonding and self-control will also be examined as dependent variables.

CHAPTER 4

Descriptive Information

INTRODUCTION

Tables in this chapter are used to display descriptive statistics for the total sample as well as for each racial group. Descriptive statistics are presented for both the predictor and the dependent variables. Percentages are presented for selected variables including race, gender, and average grade. Percentages for parental supervision are shown for each racial group. A description of factor analysis results is presented; however, the tables are included in Appendix B. Finally, mean score comparisons and correlations are provided.

Descriptive Statistics for the Full Sample

Delinquency is the primary dependent variable. Four types of offenses are used to measure delinquency: interpersonal, property, vandalism, and substance/drug use. Each type of delinquency will be analyzed for the full sample and each sub-sample by race and gender. Univariate and bivariate analyses were computed using interval level measures that indicate various levels of involvement in delinquent behavior.

In Table 4.1 descriptive statistics of the selected variables indicate that approximately 65 percent of the respondents are White, 12.8 percent are African American, and 22.2 percent are Native Americans. The sample consists of approximately 43 percent males and 56.6 percent females. The average age of the respondents is 17 and the age range is 15 to 21. The average grade on a 4-point scale is 2.61, which is approximately a C+. The mean score for the self-control scale is 62.90. Mean scores for the social bonding measures are: parental supervision, 10.35; family attachment, 2.93; school attachment, 19.55; and involvement in conventional pursuits, 45.45. Self-esteem has a mean score of 22.99. The delinquency measures have low mean scores (interpersonal, 1.65; property, 3.35; vandalism, .87, and substance/drug use, 12.54), which reflect a high number of zeros indicating no involvement in these types of delinquency offenses. Substance/drug use does have a higher mean score than the other measures of delinquency indicating more involvement for the overall sample.

Table 4.1. Descriptive Statistics of Selected Variables

Variable Description	N	Mean	SD	Min	Max
Race	1724				
(1= Indian, 0=Other)		22.2	77.8	0	1
(1=Black 0=Other)		12.8	87.2	0	1
(1= White, 0=Other)		65.1	34.9	0	1
Gender	1722	.43	56.6	0	1
(1= male, 0= female)					
Age *(years)*	1718	17	1.06	15	21
Average Grade	1719	2.61	.865	1	4
(1=D, 2=C, 3=B, 4=A)					
Self-control *(scale)*	1616	62.90	12.18	24	95
Parental super. *(scale)*	1710	10.35	1.78	3	12
Family attachment *(scale)*	1628	2.93	1.90	0	6
School attachment *(scale)*	1708	19.55	3.88	6	28
Involvement *(scale)*	1643	45.45	30.95	0	175
Self-esteem *(scale)*	1694	22.99	3.55	7	28
Interpersonal *(scale)*	1662	1.65	5.56	0	118
Property *(scale)*	1612	3.35	8.95	0	103
Vandalism *(scale)*	1658	1.87	8.78	0	255
Substance/drug *(scale)*	1656	12.54	21.6	0	140

The descriptive statistics of the selected variables for Native Americans are displayed in Table 4.2. The means of the predictor variables self-control (61.25), self-esteem (22.63), and the social bonding variables of parental supervision (10.12), family attachment (2.76), and school attachment (19.32), were lower for Native Americans than for either African Americans or Whites. The mean score for involvement in conventional pursuits (43.70) was higher than that of African Americans. In addition, the means for the delinquency measures are slightly higher than for the overall sample (interpersonal, 2.02; property, 4.28; vandalism, 2.89; and substance/drug use, 15.12).

The average age is 17.2, and the average grade is 2.43, which is less than the overall average. The Native American sample consisted of 42 percent males and 58 percent females.

Table 4.2.   Descriptive Statistics of Selected Variables for Native Americans

Variable Description	N	Mean	SD	Min	Max
Self-control (*scale*)	364	61.25	12.3	24	95
Self-esteem *(scale)*	375	22.63	3.48	7	28
Parental super. *(scale)*	378	10.12	1.97	3	12
Family attachment *(scale)*	343	2.76	1.70	0	6
School attachment *(scale)*	379	19.32	3.79	6	27
Involvement *(scale)*	364	43.70	30.9	0	175
Interpersonal *(scale)*	367	2.02	4.67	0	48
Property *(scale)*	362	4.28	12.3	0	103
Vandalism *(scale)*	368	2.89	15.9	0	255
Substance/drug *(scale)*	361	15.12	24.4	0	132
Average Grade	382	2.43	.87	1	4
(1=D, 2=C, 3=B, 4=A)					
Age	381	17.2	1.11	15	21
Gender	382	.42	58.4	1	2
(1=male, 2=female)					

Table 4.3 features descriptive statistics for African Americans. The mean score for self-control is 61.15, which is slightly lower than that of Native Americans. The mean scores for African Americans were higher than those for Native Americans for self-esteem, family attachment, school attachment, and parental supervision (only slightly), but lower for involvement in conventional pursuits. The delinquency measures for African Americans have the following means: interpersonal, 2.50; property, 3.83; vandalism, 1.58; and substance/drug use, 5.02. Compared to Native Americans, African Americans have a higher mean score for interpersonal delinquency and lower mean scores for property, vandalism and substance/drug use. The average grade point is 2.36, which ranks African Americans third out of the three ethnic groups. The average age for the African American sample is 17.2, and fewer males are included in this sample (41%) than either the Native American or the White sample.

Table 4.3. Descriptive Statistics of Selected Variables for African
            Americans

Variable Description	N	Mean	SD	Min	Max
Self-control *(scale)*	194	61.15	13.1	24	95
Self-esteem *(scale)*	212	23.39	3.71	7	28
Parental super. *(scale)*	215	10.20	2.01	3	12
Family attach. *(scale)*	196	3.13	1.72	0	6
School attach. (scale)	218	20.37	4.06	6	28
Involvement *(scale)*	199	42.96	33.9	0	168
Interpersonal *(scale)*	205	2.50	11.9	0	118
Property *(scale)*	192	3.83	7.25	0	149
Vandalism *(scale)*	205	1.58	5.32	0	159
Substance/drug *(scale)*	201	5.02	15.1	0	140
Average Grade	218	2.36	.81	1	4
(1=D, 2=C, 3=D, 4=A)					
Age	218	17.2	1.11	15	20
Gender	220	.41	59.1	1	2
(1=male, 2=female)					

Table 4.4 lists the mean scores for Whites. Whites have a higher
mean score for self-control than do either Native Americans or African
Americans. The means score of self-esteem for Whites is higher than
that for Native Americans but slightly lower than the mean score for
African Americans.   Mean scores for the social bonding measures
indicate that Whites have higher parental supervision (10.46) than
either Native Americans or African Americans; higher family
attachment (2.95) than Native Americans but lower family attachment
than African Americans; slightly higher school attachment (19.46) than
Native Americans but lower school attachment than African
Americans; and involvement in conventional pursuits is higher for
Whites than either Native Americans or African Americans. The
delinquency measures for Whites are as follows: interpersonal, 1.36;
property, 2.94; vandalism, 1.58; and substance use, 13.08.
Interpersonal and property delinquency mean scores for Whites are
lower than those of Native Americans and African Americans,
vandalism is the same as that for African Americans, and the mean
score for substance/drug use is higher than that of African Americans.

The average respondent's age is 17.09 and the average grade point is 2.73. Gender percentages for the White sample consist of 45 percent males and 55 percent females.

Table 4.4. Descriptive Statistics of Selected Variables for Whites

Variable Description	N	Mean	SD	Min	Max
Self-control (*scale*)	1058	63.79	11.9	24	95
Self-esteem *(scale)*	1107	23.03	3.54	7	28
Parental super. *(scale)*	1117	10.46	1.65	3	12
Family attach. *(scale)*	1089	2.95	1.96	0	6
School attach. *(scale)*	1111	19.46	3.86	8	28
Involvement *(scale)*	1080	46.49	30.40	0	170
Interpersonal *(scale)*	1090	1.36	3.57	0	37
Property *(scale)*	1058	2.94	7.80	0	77
Vandalism *(scale)*	1085	1.58	5.11	0	85
Substance/drug *(scale)*	1094	13.08	21.3	0	140
Average Grade	1119	2.73	.85	1	4
(1=D, 2 =C, 3=B, 4=A)					
Age	1119	17.09	1.03	15	21
Gender	1120	.45	55.5	1	2
(1=male, 2=female)					

In summary, compared to Whites, Native Americans score lower on all of the predictor measures except involvement in conventional pursuits for which there is a significant difference (Whites, 19.46 and Native Americans, 43.70). Higher mean scores indicate more social bonding, self-esteem, and self-control. Native Americans' mean scores on all of the delinquency measures were higher than Whites, indicating more involvement in delinquent activities. Whites also had the highest overall grade point average at 2.73.

The mean scores for self-control and parental supervision were lower for African Americans than for Whites. The mean scores for self-esteem, family attachment, school attachment and involvement in conventional pursuits for African Americans were higher than for Whites. Interpersonal and property delinquency mean scores were lower for Whites than for African Americans. Substance/drug use

mean scores were higher for Whites and the means scores for
vandalism were the same for both groups.

Table 4.5.   Gender (Percentage in Parentheses)

Gender	Total	Native American	African American	White
Male	747	159	90	498
	(43.4)	(41.6)	(40.9)	(44.5)
Female	975	223	130	622
	(56.6)	(58.4)	(59.1)	(55.5)
Missing	2	0	0	2
	(0.3)			(0.3)
Total	1724	382	220	1120

Table 4.6.   Age (Percentage in Parentheses)

Age	Total	Native American	African American	White
15	72	14	8	50
	(4.2)	(3.7)	(3.7)	(4.5)
16	435	97	54	284
	(25.3)	(25.5)	(24.9)	(25.4)
17	598	118	74	406
	(34.8)	(31.0)	(33.9)	(36.3)
18	437	100	53	284
	(25.4)	(26.2)	(24.3)	(25.4)
19	156	47	24	85
	(9.1)	(12.3)	(11.0)	(7.6)
20	18	4	5	9
	(1.0)	(1.0)	(2.3)	(.8
21	2	1	0	1
	(.1)	(.1)	(0)	(.1)
Missing	6	1	2	3
	(0.4)	(0.3)	(0.3)	(0.3)
Total	1724	382	220	1122

Table 4.5 indicates that 747 of the respondents in this study are
males, which comprise 43.4 percent. Of the males, 159 are Native
Americans, 90 are African Americans, and 498 are Whites. There are

975 females or 56.6 percent represented in this study. Of the females, 223 are Native Americans, 130 are African Americans, and 622 are Whites.

The age range is from 15 to 21, as shown in Table 4.6. Eighteen of the respondents are 20 years of age and two of the respondents are 21 years of age. The highest percentage of respondents (34.8) is 17 years of age.

Average grade is a control variable that is described in Table 4.7. This table shows the breakdown by letter grade of the averages for each racial group. Approximately 63 percent of White respondents held an A or B average and only 8.3 percent made a D. Approximately 46 percent of Native Americans and 44 percent of African Americans were in the A or B categories. Both African Americans and Native Americans had 14.7 percent with a D average.

Parental supervision is examined as a measure of social bonding; however, since research on this variable is so limited, especially as it relates to minorities, each component of parental supervision is also examined in Tables 4.8 - 4.10 by racial group.

Table 4.7.   Average Grade (Percentage in Parentheses)

Average Grade	Total	Native American	African American	White
4	257	42	15	200
A	(15.0)	(11.0)	(6.9)	(17.9)
3	720	135	80	505
B	(41.9)	(35.3)	(36.7)	(45.1)
2	561	149	91	321
C	(32.6)	(39.0)	(41.7)	(28.7)
1	181	56	32	93
D	(10.5)	(14.7)	(14.7)	(8.3)
Missing	5	0	2	3
	(0.3)		(0.3)	(0.3)
Total	1724	382	220	1122

Table 4.8 shows that approximately 17 percent of Native Americans agreed that they were adequately monitored. Only about 14

percent agreed that their parents recognized when they did something wrong, and 12.4 percent reported that they were disciplined when they did something wrong.

In Table 4.9 approximately 14 percent of African Americans agreed that their parents/guardians adequately monitored them when they were younger. Fifteen percent of African Americans reported that wrong behavior was recognized and that they were disciplined.

Table 4.8. Parental Supervision for Native Americans (Percentage in Parentheses)

	Monitor	Recognize	Discipline
Strongly Agree	21 (5.5)	15 (4.0)	15 (4.0)
Agree Somewhat	42 (11.1)	37 (9.8)	32 (8.4)
Disagree Somewhat	115 (30.3)	117 (31.0)	105 (27.7)
Strongly Disagree	201 (53.0)	209 (55.3)	227 (59.9)
Missing	3 (0.8)	4 (1.1)	3 (0.8)
Total	382	382	382

Approximately 11 percent of Whites in Table 4.10 agreed that they were monitored. This is less than either Native Americans or African Americans. Approximately eight percent of Whites reported that wrong behavior was recognized, and about 10 percent reported that they were disciplined.

Table 4.9. Parental Supervision for African Americans (Percentage in Parentheses)

	Monitor	Recognize	Discipline
Strongly Agree	13 (6.0)	7 (3.3)	18 (8.4)
Agree Somewhat	17 (7.9)	24 (11.2)	14 (6.5)
Disagree Somewhat	55 (25.6)	60 (27.9)	47 (21.9)
Strongly Disagree	130 (60.5)	124 (57.7)	136 (63.3)
Missing	5 (2.3)	5 (2.3)	5 (2.3)
Total	220	220	220

Table 4.10. Parental Supervision for Whites (Percentage in Parentheses)

	Monitor	Recognize	Discipline
Strongly Agree	37 (3.3)	17 (1.5)	31 (2.8)
Agree Somewhat	85 (7.6)	71 (6.4)	75 (6.7)
Disagree Somewhat	369 (33.0)	340 (30.4)	294 (26.3)
Strongly Disagree	626 (56.0)	689 (61.7)	717 (64.2)
Missing	5 (0.4)	5 (0.4)	5 (0.4)
Total	1122	1122	1122

The overall indications are that fewer Whites felt that they were monitored, their wrong behavior was recognized, or that they were disciplined, than either Native Americans or African Americans. More African Americans reported that their wrong behavior was recognized and they were disciplined, and more Native Americans agreed that they were monitored.

Factor Analysis

Defining dimensions underlying existing measurement instruments is a common use of factor analysis. Factor analysis is used to determine what items or scales should be included or excluded from a measure. It requires two stages: factor extraction and factor rotation. The primary objective of the first stage is to make an initial decision about the number of factors underlying a set of measured variables. The eigenvalue should be greater than one. The second stage is designed to accomplish two goals: (1) to statistically manipulate the results to make the factors more interpretable and (2) to make final decisions about the number of underlying factors (Green and Salkind, 2003: 297). Factor analysis is used to define indicators of constructs, to define dimensions for the measure, and to select items, which will be included on the measure. It uncovers the one-dimensional and multidimensional potential of the data.

Previous research (Arneklev et al., 1993; Grasmick et al., 1993; Wood et al., 1993; Cochran et al., 1998) has established that one-dimensional and multidimensional requirements have been met for the scale used to measure self-control. Factor analysis results for other scales are displayed in Appendix B, Tables 1 and 2. Table 1 shows factor analysis for the dependent variables and a specific scale for each of the delinquency indicators. Table 2 lists factor analysis results for self-esteem and each of the social bonding indicators. In addition, each table lists the alpha reliability score for the scale and the respective alpha score if a particular item is deleted.

Table 1 in Appendix B shows the factor analysis results for the interpersonal delinquency scale. The eigenvalue is 2.94, and Cronbach's alpha is .77. The eigenvalue for property delinquency is 2.26, and Cronbach's alpha is approximately .62. The scale is based on the acceptable criterion of *a priori* conceptual beliefs endorsed by past research using the number of factors included in the scale. The eigenvalue for the vandalism delinquency scale is 3.01 and Cronbach's alpha is .80. Factor analysis results for the substance/drug use delinquency scale indicate an eigenvalue of 3.08, and Cronbach's alpha is .74. Self-esteem's eigenvalue is 2.85, and Cronbach's alpha is .74.

Factor analysis results for parental supervision, a measure of social bonding, indicate an eigenvalue of 1.76, and Cronbach's alpha is .64. Family attachment, another measure of social bonding, has an eigenvalue of 2.49 and Cronbach's alpha is .72. The eigenvalue for school attachment, a measure of social bonding, is 3.01, and Cronbach's alpha is .80. Factor analysis results for involvement in conventional pursuits, a measure of social bonding, has an eigenvalue of 2.05 and Cronbach's alpha is .56. Those Cronbach's alphas that are less than the recommended .70 are used because they have been used in prior research or because they represent the only variables available for use in this research.

Mean Scores and Correlations

Mean scores for parental supervision are presented in Table 4.11. Each item in the scale is compared by race. Mean scores for "monitor" are 3.42 for Whites, 3.40 for African Americans and 3.31 for Native Americans. Mean scores for "recognize" are 3.52 for Whites, 3.40 for African Americans and 3.38 for Native Americans. The same pattern follows for "punished," except Native Americans have a higher mean score (3.44) than do African Americans (3.40).

Table 4.11. Mean Scores for Parental Supervision (Number of Cases in (Parentheses)

	Parental Supervision	Monitor	Recognize	Punished
Native American	10.12 (378)	3.31 (379)	3.38 (378)	3.44 (379)
African American	10.20 (215)	3.40 (215)	3.40 (215)	3.40 (215)
White	10.46 (1117)	3.42 (1117)	3.52 (1117)	3.52 (1117)

Table 4.12 features the results of t-tests of differences in mean scores for race when observing the selected predictor variables. Significant differences in means were found for Native American/White in self-control (t = -3.49, p = .001); supervision (t = -3.33, p = .001); property delinquency (t = 2.40, p = .016); interpersonal delinquency (t = 2.83, p = .005); vandalism (t = 2.37, p = .018); average grade (t = -5.89, p = .000); and age (t = 2.12, p = .034). For Native American/African American significant differences were observed for self-esteem (t = -2.48, p = .013); family attachment (t= -.2.36, p = .019); school attachment (t = -3.17, p = .002); and substance/drug use (t = 5.33, p = .000). Significant differences in means for White/African American were observed for self-control (t = -2.80, p = .005); supervision (t = -2.00, p = .046); school attachment (t = 3.17, p = .002); interpersonal delinquency (t = 2.60, p = .010); substance/drug use (t = -5.14, p = .000); and average grade (t = -5.88, p = .000).

Table 4.13 lists the Pearson's correlation coefficients for the four indicators of delinquency – property crimes, substance/drug use, interpersonal crimes, and vandalism – with social bonding, self-esteem, and self-control. There are significant negative associations between self-esteem and property crimes (-.077), self-esteem and substance/drug use (-.054), and self-esteem and vandalism (-.108). The relationship between self-esteem and interpersonal delinquency was not statistically significant. A statistically significant inverse relationship was observed between self-control and each type of delinquency: property crimes (-.349), substance/drug use (-.295), interpersonal crimes (-.345) and vandalism (-.345).

Table 4.13 also shows the associations among the four indicators of delinquency (interpersonal, property, substance/drug use, and vandalism) and the indicators of social bonding (parental supervision, family attachment, school attachment, and involvement in conventional pursuits). Statistically significant negative associations were observed among the four delinquency scales and three of the scales designed to measure social bonding. Although not strong, significant negative correlations exist in the relationship between parental supervision and the delinquency measures. The significant correlations include property (-.116), substance/drug use (-.051), interpersonal (-.049), and vandalism (-.115). None of the relationships were significant between involvement in conventional pursuits and the delinquency indicators.

The association between family attachment and the delinquency measures indicate the following: property (-.257), substance/drug use (-.227), interpersonal (-.172), and vandalism (-.241). School attachment is negatively correlated with the delinquency measures – property (-.152), substance/drug use (-.199), interpersonal (-.165), and vandalism (-.180).

The relationship between self-esteem and self-control was also found to be statistically significant (.216). In addition, self-esteem was also positively related to parental supervision (.214), and school attachment (.216). A positive correlation is observed between self-esteem and family attachment (.294). A weak significant positive association was observed between self-esteem and involvement in conventional pursuits (.101). When examining the correlation of the various measures with self-control, family attachment exhibited the strongest correlation, which is positive (.403). A statistically significant positive association was also observed between self-control and school attachment (.334). A positive association is observed between self-control and involvement in conventional pursuits (.128).

Table 4.12. T-Tests of Differences in Mean Scores for Selected Variables

	Native American/White			Native Am./ Afr.American			White/African American		
	t	Sig.	Mean Diff.	t	Sig.	Mean Diff.	t	Sig.	Mean Diff.
Self-control	-3.49	.001	-2.54	.085	.932	.095	-2.80	.005	-2.64
Self-esteem	-1.93	.054	-.406	-2.48	.013	-.760	1.33	.186	.354
Parental Supervision	-3.33	.001	-.344	-.521	.603	-.088	-2.00	.046	-.256
Family Attachment	-1.62	.106	-.192	-2.36	.019	-.372	-1.20	.229	-.180
School. Attachment	-.600	.548	-.137	-3.17	.002	-1.05	3.17	.002	.913
Involvement	-1.51	.131	-2.79	.262	.793	.738	-.760	.448	-1.04
Property	2.40	.016	1.34	.460	.646	.443	1.48	.140	.895
Interpersonal	2.83	.005	.661	-.679	.498	-.478	2.60	.010	1.14
Substance	1.53	.127	2.05	5.33	.000	10.1	-5.14	.000	-8.06
Vandalism	2.37	.018	1.31	1.15	.252	1.32	-.013	.990	-.005
Avg. Grade	-5.89	.000	-.30	.929	.353	.18	-5.88	.000	-.368
Age	2.12	.034	.133	.127	.899	.012	-1.56	.120	-.121
Gender	.966	.334	.03	-.171	.864	.01	-.971	.332	-.04

The relationships between the delinquency indicators and the social bonding measures indicate that parental supervision, family attachment, and school attachment decrease the prevalence of property delinquency, substance/drug use, interpersonal delinquency and vandalism. The most significant effects are found between family attachment and the delinquency indicators: property, substance/drug use and vandalism. These associations are fundamental to this study because they relate to Hirschi's social bonding theory. Hirschi developed social bonding theory prior to Gottfredson and Hirschi's self-control theory. The premise of this research is that social bonding precedes self-control and the significant inverse associations between the social bonding indicators and the delinquency measures are as expected except for involvement in conventional pursuits. Social bonding emphasizes the role of the family and parenting; therefore, these associations are very important to the overall purpose of this study.

The initial data analyses warrant further multivariate analysis. The data indicate statistically significant negative associations between each delinquency indicator and self-control, which suggest that self-control decreases the prevalence of delinquency. These findings are supported by other research reporting an inverse relationship between self-control and delinquency (Gottfredson and Hirschi, 1990; Grasmick et al., 1993; Wood et al., 1993; Arneklev et al., 1993). Self-esteem has a weak negative association with several of the delinquency indicators, and no significance is found in the association between self-esteem and interpersonal delinquency. These findings are not encouraging; however, since researchers (Kaplan, 1982; Wells and Rankin, 1983; McCarthy and Hoge, 1984; Wells, 1989; Rosenberg et al., 1989) are still debating the relationship between self-esteem and delinquency it is not surprising that the findings are not clearly indicating an association. Rosenberg et al. (1989) address the weak bivariate relationship between self-esteem and delinquency by attributing it to the countervailing effect of the two variables, in which high self-esteem lowers delinquency and high delinquency increases self-esteem. The data also indicate a positive association between self-control and self-esteem. The question of causal order can be addressed by further investigation into this relationship.

Table 4.13.   Correlation Matrix, Full Sample

	Interper. Deling.	Prop. Deling.	Vandal. Deling.	Substance Deling.	Self-Control	Self-Esteem	Parental Super.	Family Attach.	School Attach.
Interper. Deling.									
Prop. Delinq.	.310**								
Vandal. Delinq.	.337**	.412**							
Substance Delinq.	.274**	.300**	.242**						
Self-Control	-.345**	-.349**	-.345**	-.295**					
Self-Esteem	-045	-.077**	-.108**	-.054*	.216**				
Parental Super.	-.049**	-.116**	-.115**	-.051*	.063*	.214**			
Family Attach.	-.172**	-.257**	-.241**	-.227**	.403**	.294**	.145**		
School Attach.	-.165**	-.152**	-.180**	-.199**	.334**	.216**	.176**	.329**	
Involvement	-.024	.032	.016	-.029	.128**	.101**	.083**	.063*	-.133**
Native Amer.	.094**	.043*	.049*	.051	-.073**	-.054	-.071**	-.052*	-.031
African Amer.	.014	.064*	-.017	-.132**	-.053*	.043	-.031	.039	.081**
Whites	-.092**	-.081**	-.030	.046	.101**	.018	.083**	.014	-.030
Males	.161**	.151**	.157**	.018	-.119**	.072**	-.070**	.091**	.100**
Avg. grade	-.177**	-.182**	-.140**	-.190**	.340**	.241**	.099**	.205**	.278**
Age	-.022	-078**	-.054*	.051*	.078*	.088**	.033	.045	-.025

Table 4.13. (cont'd)

	Convent. Pursuits	Native Amer.	African Amer.	White	Male	Female	Avg. Grade	Age
Convent. Pursuits	—							
Native Amer.	-.030	—						
African Amer.	-.030	-.204**	—					
White	.047	-.728**	-.522**	—				
Male	-019**	-019	-.019	.030	—			
Average grade	.182**	-.115**	-.112**	.179**	-.059*	.059*	—	
Age	-.084**	-044	.027	-.057*	.109**	-.109**	-.057*	—

** p<.01, *p<.05

CHAPTER 5

Findings for Full Sample

This chapter presents the logistic regression results for the full sample. All predictor variables including race and gender are entered into a logistic regression model. Findings for the relationships between predictor variables and each delinquency measure are examined. Four models are used to show the results of the logistic regression analysis for each measure of delinquency. Model 1 includes only the control variables; the social bonding measures are added in Model 2; self-esteem is added in Model 3; and self-control is added in Model 4. A summary of the results for the models is also given.

Results for Logistic Regression Models

Logistic regression was used to analyze relationships in four models for the full sample. Model 1 examines the relationship between the control variables – race, age, gender and average grade – and each delinquency indicator. In Model 2 social bonding is added to the control variables. Social bonding is measured by parental supervision, family attachment, school attachment and involvement in conventional pursuits. Model 3 includes the control variables, the social bonding measures and self-esteem. Model 4 consists of all of the predictors including self-control.

Table 5.1 presents the logistic regression model results for predictor variables in the full sample in relationship to interpersonal delinquency. The significant relationships in Model 1 include Native American (B = .476, p<.05), average grade (B = -.418, p<.05), age (B = -.134, p<.05), and female (B = -.714, p<.05). Native Americans are 61 percent more likely to be involved in interpersonal delinquency than Whites. A unit increase in average grade decreases the likelihood of interpersonal delinquency by about 34 percent. As individuals grow older they are less likely to be involved in interpersonal delinquency, because a unit increase in age decreases the likelihood of interpersonal delinquency by 12 percent. Females are 51 percent less likely to participate in interpersonal delinquency.

Model 2 presents the relationships for the interpersonal delinquency indicators, the control variables and the social bonding indicators. The significant relationships include: Native American (B= .511, p<.05), African American (B= .292, p<.05), average grade (B= -.282, p<.05), age (B= -.132, p<.05), female (B= -.789, p<.05), school attachment (B= -.053, p<.05), and family attachment (B= -.172, p<.05).

Native Americans are 67 percent more likely to participate in interpersonal delinquency than Whites. Adding the social bonding indicators to the control variables produced significant findings for African Americans. In Model 2 African Americans are 34 percent more likely to commit interpersonal delinquency than Whites, whereas in Model 1 the relationship was not significant. Only two of the four social bonding indicators were found to be significant in Model 2, school attachment and family attachment. A one-unit increase in school attachment decreases the likelihood of interpersonal delinquency by five percent, and a unit increase in family attachment decreases the likelihood of interpersonal delinquency by 16 percent.

The relationship of interpersonal delinquency with the control variables, the social bonding indicators, and self-esteem is displayed in Model 3 of Table 5.1. Significant relationships were found for interpersonal delinquency and the following predictors: Native American (B= .514, p<.05), average grade (B= -.303, p<.05), age (B= -.143, p<.05), female (B= -.776, p<.05), family attachment (B= -.185, p<.05), and school attachment (B= -.056, p<.05). Although self-esteem is not significant when it is added in Model 3, it attenuates the significance of African American, which was observed in Model 2. The effects of the other variables remained about the same.

Native Americans are 67 percent more likely to be involved in interpersonal delinquency than Whites. A one-unit increase in average grade decreases the likelihood of interpersonal delinquency by 26 percent. A one-unit increase in age decreases the likelihood of interpersonal delinquency by approximately 13 percent. School and family attachment also have an inverse effect on interpersonal delinquency. A one-unit increase in school attachment decreases the likelihood of interpersonal delinquency by about five percent. Family attachment has a greater impact on delinquency than school attachment with a one-unit increase resulting in approximately a 17 percent decrease in the likelihood of interpersonal delinquency.

Table 5.1. Logistic Regression of Interpersonal Delinquency (Odds-Ratio in Parentheses)

	Model 1 β	Model 2 β	Model 3 β	Model 4 β
African	.161	.292*	.274	120a
American	(1.175)	(1.339)	(1.316)	(1.127)
Average Grade	-.418*	-.282*	-.303*	-.164*
	(.659)	(.755)	(.739)	(.849)
Age	-.134*	-.132*	-.143*	-.067
	(.875)	(.876)	(.867)	(.935)
Female [a]	-.714*	-.789*	-.776*	-.629*
	(.490)	(.454)	(.460)	(.533)
Parental		.013	.003	-.014
Supervision		(1.013)	(1.003)	(.986)
Family		-.172*	-.185*	-.083*
Attachment		(.842)	(.831)	(.920)
School		-.053*	-.056*	-.025
Attachment		(.948)	(.946)	(.976)
Involvement		.001	.001	.003
		(1.001)	(1.001)	(1.003)
Self-Esteem			.031	.039*
			(1.032)	(1.039)
Self-Control				-.059*
				(.943)
Constant	3.085*	4.035*	3.750*	4.728*
	(21.861)	(56.568)	(42.536)	(113.073)
Chi-square	97.580*	146.956*	150.090*	1630.057*
df	5	9	10	11
-2Log Likelihood	1779.723	1730.347	1727.213	1630.057
Cox&Snell NR^2	.07/.09	.10/.13	.10/.14	.16/.22
N	1442	1442	1442	1442

*p<.05, [a] reference category = male,   reference category = White

Model 4 displays the results of logistic regression for interpersonal delinquency and all of the predictors. Self-control is added to the other predictors and it is significant. A one-unit increase in self-control decreases the likelihood of interpersonal delinquency by approximately a five percent. There were attenuating effects of self-control on the predictor variables, which diminished the impact for some and reversed the impact for others. Though not significant, the relationship between parental supervision and interpersonal delinquency was reversed from positive to negative. Age and school attachment lost their significance as they relate to interpersonal delinquency. Although still significant, the impact of each of the other predictors was not as strong once self-control was entered into the model. Self-esteem is now positively significant.

Property delinquency logistic regression model results for the control variables and other predictors are given in Table 5.2. In Model 1 all of the control variables are significantly related to property delinquency, except Native American. The significant relationship findings include African American (B= .452, p<.05), average grade (B= -.461, p<.05), age (B= -.160, p<.05), and female (B= -.587, p<.05).

African Americans are 57 percent more likely to commit property delinquency than are Whites. A one-unit increase in average grade decreases the likelihood of property delinquency by 37 percent. A one-unit increase in age decreases the likelihood of property delinquency by 15 percent, and being female decreases the likelihood of property delinquency by 44 percent.

Model 2 in Table 5.2 lists the property delinquency logistic regression relationships between the control variables and the social bonding indicators. The significant relationships include African American (B= .569, p<.05), average grade (B = -.331, p<.05), age (B= -.143, p<.05), female (B= -.708, p<.05), parental supervision (B= -.075, p<.05), family attachment (B= -.264, p<.05), school attachment (B=-.030, p<.05), and involvement in conventional pursuits (B= .006, p<.05).

All of the predictors are significant in Model 2 except Native American. Each social bonding indicator was found to be significant. African Americans are 77 percent more likely to be involved in property delinquency than are Whites. A one-unit increase in parental supervision decreases the likelihood of property delinquency by seven percent.

Table 5.2. Logistic Regression of Property Delinquency
Odds-Ratio in Parentheses)

	Model 1 β	Model 2 β	Model 3 β	Model 4 β
Native American	.204	.185	.187	.105
	(1.227)	(1.204)	(1.206)	(1.111)
African American	.452*	.569*	.556*	.444*
	(1.572)	(1.766)	(1.744)	(1.560)
Average Grade	-.461*	-.331*	-.346*	-.215*
	(.630)	(.718)	(.707)	(.807)
Age	-.160*	-.143*	-.151*	-.087
	(.852)	(.867)	(-.860)	(.917)
Female [a]	-.587*	-.708*	-.698*	-.558*
	(.556)	(.493)	(.498)	(.572)
Parental Supervision		-.075*	-.083*	-.105*
		(.928)	(.920)	(.900)
Family Attachment		-.264*	-.273*	-.191*
		(.768)	(.761)	(.826)
School Attachment		-.030*	-.033*	-.004
		(.970)	(.968)	(.996)
Involvement		.006*	.005*	.007*
		(1.006)	(1.005)	(1.007)
Self-Esteem			.023	.029
			(1.023)	(1.030)
Self-Control				-.052*
				(.949)
Constant	4.029*	5.336*	5.138*	6.126*
	(56.193)	(207.661)	(170.358)	(457.811)
Chi-square	93.185*	192.025*	193.723*	272.433*
df	5	9	10	11
-2Log Likelihood	1839.567	1740.728	1739.029	1660.319
Cox & Snell R²/ Nagelkerke R²	.06/.09	.13/.17	.13/.17	18/.24
N	1405	1405	1405	1405

*p<.05, [a] reference category = male,   reference category = White

A one-unit increase in school attachment decreases the likelihood of property delinquency by three percent, and a one-unit increase in family attachment decreases the likelihood of property delinquency by approximately 23 percent. Involvement in conventional pursuits is significant, but the relationship is positive instead of the predicted negative relationship. A one-unit increase in involvement in conventional pursuits increases the likelihood of property delinquency by approximately one percent.

The logistic regression findings for property delinquency, the control variables, the social bonding measures and self-esteem are shown in Model 3 of Table 5.2. The significant relationships include those between property delinquency and the following predictors: African American (B=.556, p<.05), average grade (B=-.346, p<.05), age (B=-.151, p<.05), female (B= -.698, p<.05), parental supervision (B=-.083, p<.05), family attachment (B=-.273, p<.05), school attachment (B= -.033, p<.05), and involvement in conventional pursuits (B=.005, p<.05).

African Americans are approximately 74 percent more likely to participate in property delinquency than Whites. Each of the control variables, average grade, age, and gender has the expected inverse effect on property delinquency. In addition, all of the social bonding measures are significant in this model. A one-unit increase in parental supervision results in about an eight percent increase in the likelihood of property delinquency. A one-unit increase in family attachment decreases the likelihood of property delinquency by 24 percent. A one-unit increase in school attachment results in a three percent decrease in the likelihood of property delinquency. A positive relationship exists between involvement in conventional pursuits and property delinquency. A one-unit increase in involvement in conventional pursuits results in less than a one percent increase in the likelihood of property delinquency.

Like interpersonal delinquency, age and school attachment lost their significance as they relate to property delinquency once self-control was added to the model. Although still significant, the impacts of the other predictors were not as strong in the model with self-control. A one-unit increase in self-control decreases the likelihood of property delinquency by approximately five percent.

Table 5.3 displays the logistic regression results for the relationships between vandalism, the control variables, and the other independent variables. The significant relationships in Model 1 include average grade (B=-.356, p<.05), age (B=-.158, p<.05), and female (B= -.656, p<.05). A one-unit increase in average grade decreases the likelihood of vandalism by 30 percent. A one-unit increase in age decreases the likelihood of vandalism by 15 percent. Females are 48 percent less likely to be involved in vandalism than males. Race has no significance in relation to vandalism in this model.

The logistic regression results for vandalism, the control variables, and the social bonding variables are shown in Model 2 of Table 5.3. The significant relationships include average grade (B=-.167, p<.05), age (B=-.152, p<.05), female (B=-.792, p<.05), parental supervision (B=-.090, p<.05), family attachment (B=-.278, p<.05), school attachment (B= -.058, p<.05), and involvement in conventional pursuits (B=.004, p<.05).

Average grade, age and gender are the same control variables that were significant in Model 1. Race is not significant in Model 1 or Model 2. Each of the social bonding indicators is significant in this model, although a positive relationship is again observed for involvement in conventional pursuits instead of the predicted negative relationship. A one-unit increase in parental supervision decreases the likelihood of vandalism by nine percent; a unit increase in school attachment decreases the likelihood of vandalism by six percent; and a one-unit increase in family attachment decreases the likelihood of vandalism by 24 percent. For each one-unit increase of involvement in conventional pursuits the likelihood of vandalism increases by less than a half percent.

Model 3 in Table 5.3 shows the logistic regression results for vandalism, the control variables, the social bonding predictors and self-esteem. Self-esteem is not significant and it has almost no additional effect on the findings in Model 2, without self-esteem. The significant relationships include those between vandalism and average grade (B=-.162, p<.05), age (B=-.150, p<.05), female (B=-.795, p<.05), parental supervision (B= -.088, p<.05), school attachment (B=-.058, p<.05), family attachment (B=-.276, p<.05), and involvement in conventional pursuits (B=.004, p<.05).

Gender, family attachment, average grade and age have the greatest impact on decreasing the likelihood of vandalism, in that order. Females are 55 percent less likely to participate in vandalism than males. A one-unit increase in family attachment decreases the likelihood of vandalism by 24 percent; a one-unit increase in average grade decreases the likelihood of vandalism by 15 percent, and a one-unit increase in age decreases the likelihood of vandalism by 14 percent. There is also an inverse relationship between parental supervision and vandalism as well as between school attachment and vandalism; a one-unit increase in parental supervision decreases the likelihood of vandalism by eight percent, and a one-unit increase in school attachment decreases the likelihood of vandalism by approximately six percent. Involvement in conventional pursuits has a slightly positive effect on vandalism. A one-unit increase in involvement in conventional pursuits increases the likelihood of vandalism by less than one-half of one percent.

In Model 4 of Table 5.3, school attachment, age, and average grade are no longer significant when self-control is added to the model. The effect of parental supervision is enhanced slightly by adding self-control to the model. A one-unit increase in parental supervision now decreases the likelihood of vandalism by 10 percent. A one-unit increase in self-control decreases the likelihood of vandalism by approximately six percent. Adding self-control to this model also affects significance for self-esteem. A one-unit increase in self-esteem decreases the likelihood of vandalism by about one-half percent.

Logistic regression results for the relationship between substance/drug use and the control variables are presented in Model 1 of Table 5.4. Significant relationships were found between vandalism and African American (B=-.965, p<.05), average grade (B=-.527, p<.05), and age (B=.102, p<.05). African Americans are 62 percent less likely to use substance/drugs than Whites. A negative relationship was observed between grades and the likelihood of substance/drug use. A one-unit increase in grade point average decreases the likelihood of substance/drug use by 41 percent. A one-unit increase in age increases the likelihood of substance/drug use by 11 percent. There is no significant gender difference in substance/drug use.

Table 5.3.   Logistic Regression of Vandalism (Odds-Ratio in Parentheses)

	Model 1 β	Model 2 β	Model 3 β	Model 4 β
Native American	.111 (1.117)	.115 (1.122)	.115 (1.122)	.005 (1.005)
African American	-.159 (.853)	-.008 (.992)	-.005 (.995)	-.180 (.836)
Average Grade	-.356* (.700)	-.167* (.847)	-.162* (.850)	-.007 (.993)
Age	-.158* (.854)	-.152* (.859)	-.150* (.861)	-.076 (.927)
Female [a]	-.656* (.519)	-.792* (.453)	-.795* (.452)	-.645* (.525)
Parental Supervision		-.090* (.914)	-.088* (.916)	-.109* (.897)
Family Attachment		-.278* (.757)	-.276* (.759)	-.184* (.832)
School Attachment		-.058* (.944)	-.058* (.944)	-.027 (.973)
Involvement		.004* (1.004)	.004* (1.004)	.006* (1.006)
Self-Esteem			-.007 (.993)	-.003* (.997)
Self-Control				-.059* (.943)
Constant	3.199* (24.502)	5.288* (197.957)	5.350* (210.695)	6.451* (633.640)
Chi-square	65.285*	176.069*	176.211*	263.463*
df	5	9	10	11
-2Log Likelihood	1706.947	1596.162	1596.021	1508.768
Cox&SnellR²/ Nagelkerke R²	.04/.06	.12/.16	.12/.16	.17/.24
N	1435	1435	1435	1435

*p<.05, [a] reference category = male,   reference category = White

Table 5.4.   Logistic Regression of Substance/Drug Use (Odds-Ratio in Parentheses)

	Model 1 β	Model 2 β	Model 3 β	Model 4 β
	-.033	-.053	-.054	-.113
	(.968)	(.948)	(.947)	(.893)
African American	-.965*	-.895*	-.932*	-1.102*
	(.381)	(.409)	(.394)	(.332)
Average Grade	-.527*	-.381*	-.418*	-.308*
	(.591)	(.683)	(.658)	(.735)
Age	.102*	.118*	.103*	.170*
	(1.107)	(1.125)	(1.108)	(1.185)
Female [a]	-.032	-.079	-.060	.097
	(.969)	(.924)	(.942)	(1.102)
Parental Supervision		-.030	-.048	-.063*
		(.970)	(.953)	(.939)
Family Attachment		-.195*	-.215*	-.139*
		(.823)	(.807)	(.870)
School Attachment		-.054*	-.059*	-.036*
		(.948)	(.943)	(.965)
Involvement		.001	.001	.001
		(1.001)	(1.001)	(1.001)
Self-Esteem			.051*	.058*
			(1.052)	(1.060)
Self-Control				-.043*
				(.958)
Constant	.124	1.409*	.953	1.455
	(1.132)	(4.094)	(2.594)	(4.285)
Chi-square	93.710*	163.669*	172.250*	230.591*
df	5	9	10	11
-2 Log Likelihood	1899.698	1829.738	1821.158	1762.816
Cox & Snell R²/ Nagelkerke R²	.06/.08	.11/.14	.11/.15	.15/.20
N	1463	1463	1463	1463

*p<.05, [a] reference category = male,   reference category = White

Logistic regression results for substance/drug use, the control variables and the social bonding indicator are presented in Model 2 of Table 5.4. The significant relationships include those for African American (B=-.895, p<.05), average grade (B=-.381, p<.05), age (B= .118, p<.05), family attachment (B=-.195, p<.05), and school attachment (B=-.054, p<.05). The same control variables that were significant in Model 1 are also significant in Model 2. In addition, two of the social bonding indicators, family attachment and school attachment, were found to decrease the likelihood of substance/ drug use. A one-unit increase in family attachment results in an 18 percent decrease in the likelihood of substance/drug use, and a one-unit increase in school attachment results in a five percent decrease in the likelihood of substance/drug use.

Model 3 in Table 5.4 presents the logistic regression results for substance/drug use as it relates to the control variables, the social bonding predictors and self-esteem. Self-esteem has a significant impact on substance/drug use when added to this model (B=.051, p<.05); however, that impact is positive. A one-unit increase in self-esteem increases the likelihood of substance/drug use by about five percent. The impact of the other variables remained about the same as they were in Model 2 before self-esteem was added to the model.

Model 4 lists the results for substance/drug use in relation to all of the predictors including self-control. The most significant change is found in the effects of parental supervision (B=-.063, p<.05) on substance/drug use. A one-unit increase in parental supervision decreases the likelihood of substance/drug use by six percent. There was no significance in the relationship between parental supervision and substance/drug use until self-control was added to the model. A one-unit increase in self-esteem decreases the likelihood of substance/drug use by approximately four percent.

Summary of Logistic Regression Model Results

Table 5.5 summarizes the findings for each delinquency measure. Model 1 presents the significant findings for each of the delinquency measures and the control variables – race, average grade, age, and gender. White is the reference category for race and male is the reference category for gender. Interpersonal delinquency is significantly affected by average grade, age, being female, and Native

American but not African American. Property delinquency is significantly affected by African American, average grade, age and female. Vandalism is significantly impacted by average grade, age and gender. Substance/drug use is significantly affected by African American, average grade, and age, but not gender. In terms of race, Native Americans have greater involvement in interpersonal delinquency than are Whites. Native Americans and African Americans are more likely to commit property delinquency than do Whites. No racial significance was found for vandalism. African Americans are less likely to be involved in substance/drug use than are Whites.

Model 2 shows the effects of adding the social bonding indicators to the control variables for each measure of delinquency. The impact on interpersonal delinquency remains the same, except for the significance of race. African Americans now show significance and are more likely to engage in interpersonal delinquency than are Whites. The effects of the social bonding indicators on property delinquency, vandalism and substance/drug use do not change the impact of the control variables. In addition, the social bonding indicators have the same effect on interpersonal delinquency and substance/drug use. Family attachment and school attachment have significant negative effects on interpersonal delinquency and substance/drug use delinquency. No significance was found for the effect of parental supervision and involvement in conventional pursuits as they relate to interpersonal delinquency and substance/drug use delinquency. The effects of the social bonding indicators on property delinquency and vandalism are also the same. Parental supervision, family attachment, and school attachment all have significant inverse effects on property delinquency and vandalism. The presence of these three indicators significantly decreases the likelihood of involvement in property delinquency and vandalism. Involvement in conventional pursuits is significant for both property delinquency and vandalism; however, the effect is positive. Therefore, the likelihood of involvement in these two types of delinquency increases when individuals are engaged in conventional pursuits.

Model 3 shows the results of adding self-esteem to the control variables and the social bonding indicators. Although the effect of self-esteem is not significant, being African American is no longer significant in Model 3 for interpersonal delinquency. The significant effect of being Native American remains the same for interpersonal delinquency but drops off for the other three delinquency indicators when self-esteem is added to the model.

Model 4 examines the impact of self-control. Self-control attenuates the effects of age and family attachment on interpersonal delinquency. Both age and family attachment fail to maintain their significance when self-control is added to the model. Self-esteem now has a positive effect on interpersonal delinquency with self-control in the model. Self-control also attenuates the effects of school attachment on property delinquency and vandalism. School attachment is no longer significant for either property delinquency or vandalism. In addition, average grade and age no longer have a significant impact on vandalism. Parental supervision becomes significant in its effect on substance/drug use when self-control is added.

Overall, the social bonding indicators that have the most significant impact on delinquency are family attachment and school attachment. Parental supervision significantly decreases the likelihood of property delinquency and vandalism but not interpersonal delinquency, and substance/drug use is significantly decreased only when self-control is added. Self-esteem does not decrease the likelihood of any of the delinquency measures, but it increases the likelihood of interpersonal delinquency when self-control is added. Self-esteem also positively affects substance/drug use. Self-control is significant across each type of delinquency, decreasing the likelihood of involvement in delinquency.

Table 5.5.   Summary of Logistic Regression Significant Model Results

Predictors	Interpersonal Delinquency Models				Property Delinquency Models				Vandalism Delinquency Models				Substance/Drug Delinquency Models			
	1	2	3	4	1	2	3	4	1	2	3	4	1	2	3	4
Native Am.°	+	+	+	+												
African American°		+	+	+	+	+	+	+							−	−
Average Grade		−	−	−	−	−	−	−							−	−
Age		−	−	−							−		+	+	+	+
Female[a]	−	−	−	−	−	−	−	−	−	−	−	−				
Parental Supervision		−	−	−					−	−	−	−	−	−	−	−
Family Attachment		−	−	−						−	−	−	−	−	−	−
School Attachment		−	−	−						−	−	−				
Involvement						+	+	+		+	+	+	+	+	+	+
Self-Esteem				+											+	+
Self-Control				−				−				−				−

[a] reference category = male, ° reference category = White, (+ and − signs denote the relationship between each predictor and each type of delinquency)

CHAPTER 6

Findings for Native Americans

INTRODUCTION

This chapter presents the multivariate sample results for Native Americans. First, the results of the logistic regression analysis of the relationships between the predictor variables and each measure of delinquency are discussed. Next, OLS regression results are discussed using all of the predictor variables and observing their relationships to each measure of delinquency. Since these analyses are across delinquency types, it is not necessary to hold the sample size constant; therefore, the total number varies.

Logistic Regression

Tables 6.1 - 6.4 show the logistic regression analyses of the four delinquency measures for Native Americans. Interpersonal delinquency produced significant findings for family attachment (B=-.176, p<.05), self-control (B = -.031, p<.05), and female (B=-.857, p<.05). Property delinquency produced significant findings for parental supervision (B=-.258, p<.05), family attachment (B=-.232, p<.05), involvement in conventional pursuits (B=.009, p<.05), and self-control (B=-.063, p<.05). The significant findings for vandalism include parental supervision (B=-.182, p<.05), self-control (B=-.069, p<.05), and female (B=-.614, p<.05). Significant findings for substance/drug use are parental supervision (B=-.163, p<.05), family attachment (B=-.181, p<.05), involvement in conventional pursuits (B= -.016, p<.05), self-control (B= -.037, p<.05), and self-esteem (B = .085, p<.05).

65

Table 6.1. Logistic Regression, Interpersonal Delinquency, Native
           American Sample

	B	S.E.	Wald	Sig.†	Odds-Ratio
Parental	-.031	.069	.206	.325	.969
Family Attach	-.176*	.086	4.204	.020	.838
School Attach	-.013	.037	.122	.364	.987
Involvement	.002	.004	.221	.319	1.002
Self-Esteem	.042	.041	1.012	.157	1.042
Self-Control	-.031*	.012	6.583	.005	.969
Avg. Grade	-.238	.156	2.340	.063	.788
Age	-.166	.117	2.036	.077	.847
Female [a]	-.857*	.270	10.054	.001	.425
Constant	5.792	2.244	6.660	.050	327.533
Chi-square	44.359				
Chi-square sig.	.000				
df	9				
-2 Log	378.85				
Likelihood	9				
Cox & Snell R^2/ Nagelkerke R^2	.13/.18				
N	308				

*$p<.05$, † one-tailed significance level, [a] reference category = male

The relationship between parental supervision and delinquency is
significant for property delinquency, vandalism and substance/drug use.
A one-unit increase in parental supervision results in a 23 percent
decrease in the likelihood of property delinquency for Native
Americans. A one-unit increase in parental supervision also results in
approximately a 16 percent decrease in vandalism for Native
Americans. Family attachment was significant for three of the
measures. A one-unit increase in family attachment results in a 16
percent decrease in the likelihood of interpersonal delinquency; a 20
percent decrease in the likelihood of property delinquency; a 14 percent
decline in the likelihood of vandalism, and a 16 percent decrease in the
likelihood of substance/drug use for Native Americans.

Table 6.2.   Logistic Regression, Property Delinquency, Native American Sample

	B	S.E.	Wald	Sig. †	Odds-Ratio
Parental	-.258*	.076	11.431	.001	.773
Family Attach	-.232*	.092	6.308	.006	.793
School Attach	.003	.040	.004	.475	1.003
Involvement	.009*	.005	3.819	.026	1.009
Self-Esteem	.011	.044	.063	.401	1.011
Self-Control	-.063*	.014	21.554	.000	.939
Avg. Grade	-.187	.169	1.223	.135	.829
Age	-.152	.126	1.460	.114	.859
Female ᵃ	-.396	.293	1.826	.089	.673
Constant	9.717	2.493	15.189	.000	16590.586
Chi-square	88.286				
Chi-square sig.	.000				
df	9				
-2 Log Likelihood	335.711				
Cox&Snell R²/ Nagelkerke R²	.25/.33				
N	306				

*p<.05, † one-tailed significance level, ᵃ reference category = male

Involvement in conventional pursuits has an unexpected positive effect on property delinquency for Native Americans. A one-unit increase in involvement in conventional pursuits results in about a one percent increase in the likelihood of property delinquency. Native American individuals who were involved in conventional pursuits were slightly less likely to use substances/drugs. A one-unit increase in involvement in conventional pursuits resulted in about a two percent decrease in substance/drug use.

Self-control is significant for each of the delinquency measures. A one-unit increase in self control results in about a three percent decrease in the likelihood of interpersonal delinquency, a six percent decrease in the likelihood of property delinquency, a seven percent decrease in the likelihood of vandalism and a four percent decrease in the likelihood of substance/drug use for Native Americans.

A slightly positive relationship exists for self-esteem and substance/drug use among Native Americans. A one-unit increase in self-esteem results in a nine percent increase in the likelihood of substance/drug use. Gender differences were significant for interpersonal delinquency and vandalism. Native American females are 57 percent less likely to be involved in interpersonal delinquency than Native American males, and they are 46 percent less likely to commit vandalism than Native American males. No significant gender differences were found for Native Americans in relation to property and substance/drug use.

Table 6.3.   Logistic Regression, Vandalism, Native American Sample

	B	S.E.	Wald	Sig.†	Odds-Ratio
Parental	-.182*	.073	6.183	.007	.834
Family Attach	-.147	.094	2.450	.059	.863
School Attach	.038	.042	.824	.182	1.039
Involvement	.006	.004	1.531	.108	1.006
Self-Esteem	-.055	.044	1.576	.105	.947
Self-Control	-.069*	.014	23.705	.000	.933
Avg. Grade	.080	.172	.217	.321	1.083
Age	-.056	.127	.190	.332	.946
Female [a]	-.614*	.292	4.428	.018	.541
Constant	7.027	2.502	7.890	.003	1127.154
Chi-square	66.538				
Chi-square sig.	.000				
df	9				
-2 Log Likelihood	326.199				
Cox&Snell R²/ Nagelkerke R²	.20/.28				
N	309				

*p<.05, † one-tailed significance level, [a] reference category = male

Table 6.4. Logistic Regression, Substance/Drug Use, Native American
Sample

	B	S.E.	Wald	Sig.†	Odds-Ratio
Parental	-.163*	.076	4.613	.032	.850
Family Attach	-.181*	.087	4.315	.038	.835
School Attach	-.010	.037	.078	.780	.990
Involvement	-.016*	.008	4.244	.039	.984
Self-Esteem	.085*	.043	3.987	.046	1.089
Self-Control	-.037*	.012	8.784	.003	.964
Avg. Grade	-.220	.159	1.918	.166	.802
Age	.000	.119	.000	1.00	1.000
Female [a]	.014	.274	.002	.480	1.014
Constant	4.039	2.261	3.190	.037	56.749
Chi-square	44.904				
Chi-square sig.	.000				
df	9				
-2 Log Likelihood	370.859				
Cox & Snell R^2/ Nagelkerke R^2	.13/.18				
N	313				

*$p<.05$, † one-tailed significance level, [a] reference category = male

OLS REGRESSION

OLS regression results of interpersonal delinquency for Native Americans are listed in Table 6.5. Only one predictor variable, self-control, was found to be significant in this model. Self-control has a significant inverse effect (B= -.096, p= .000) on interpersonal delinquency. Gender is the only control variable that was significant for Native Americans. Females are less likely to participate in interpersonal delinquency than are males (B=-1.513, p=.003). Other predictors that were negatively associated with interpersonal delinquency but were not significant include parental supervision, family attachment, and school attachment. Approximately 14 percent of the variation in interpersonal delinquency for Native Americans can be attributed to the variables in this model.

The Effects of Race and Family Attachment

OLS property delinquency regression results for Native Americans are given in Table 6.6. The significant predictors are family attachment, school attachment, and self-control. Family attachment has a negative effect (B=-1.239, p=.045) on property delinquency. An inverse effect was also produced by school attachment (B=-.374, p=.029). The significant relationship between involvement in conventional pursuits and property delinquent is positive (B=.060, p= .035). Involvement in conventional pursuits increases property delinquency for Native Americans. Gender (female), a control variable, was also significant. Native American females are less likely to commit property delinquency than Native American males (B=-3.492, p= .010). An inverse effect was produced by self-control (B=-.143, p= .014). Parental supervision and average grade were in the expected direction but the findings were not significant. The total effect of the predictor and control variables in this model accounts for 16 percent (r^2 = .16) of the variance in property delinquency for Native Americans.

Table 6.5.   OLS Regression, Full Model, Interpersonal Delinquency, Native American

	B	S.E.	β	t	Sig.†
Parental	-.124	.140	-.052	-.889	.188
Family Attach	-.273	.171	-.105	-1.598	.056
School Attach	-.058	.074	-.047	-.784	.217
Involvement	.012	.008	.080	1.466	.072
Self-Esteem	.024	.081	.019	.302	.382
Self-Control	-.096*	.024	-.264	-4.047	.000
Avg. Grade	.456	.310	.086	1.473	.071
Age	.296	.232	.073	1.275	.102
Female [a]	-1.513*	.537	-.159	-2.820	.003
Constant	4.698	4.412		1.065	.144
r^2	.142				
Adjusted r^2	.116				
N	307				

*p<.05, †one-tailed significance level, [a] reference category = male

Table 6.6.   OLS Regression, Full Model, Property Delinquency, Native American

	B	S.E.	β	t	Sig.†
Parental	-.280	.376	-.083	-.744	.229
Family Attach	-1.239*	.469	-.173	-2.640	.045
School Attach	-.374*	.196	-.111	-1.909	.029
Involvement	.060*	.022	.148	2.739	.035
Self-Esteem	.233	.220	.064	1.061	.145
Self-Control	-.143*	.064	-.143	-2.223	.014
Avg. Grade	-1.217	.855	-.083	-1.424	.078
Age	.271	.643	.024	.422	.337
Female [a]	-3.492*	1.482	-.133	-2.356	.010
Constant	19.414	12.150		1.596	.056
r^2	.16				
Adjusted r^2	.13				
N	305				

*p<.05, †one-tailed significance level, [a] reference category = male

OLS regression results for Native American vandalism are presented in Table 6.7. The predictors that significantly affected vandalism for Native Americans are involvement in conventional pursuits and self-control. Involvement in conventional pursuits continues to be significant in the unexpected positive direction (B= .074, p= .009). Self-control has a negative effect (B= -.204, p= .013) on vandalism. Other predictors were in the expected direction, but they were not significant. Average grade is the only control variable that is significant in this model (B= -2.137, p= .039). Together the variables in this model account for approximately nine percent of the variance in vandalism for Native Americans (r^2 = .093).

Table 6.7.   OLS Regression, Full Model, Vandalism
                   Delinquency, Native American

	B	S.E.	β	t	Sig.†
Parental	-.811	.531	-091	-1.526	.064
Family Attach	-.209	.650	-.022	-.322	.374
School Attach	-.448	.283	-.096	-1.581	.058
Involvement	.074*	.031	.134	2.398	.009
Self-Esteem	.247	.306	.050	.805	.211
Self-Control	-.204*	.091	-.151	-2.250	.013
Avg. Grade	-2.137*	1.205	-.107	-1.774	.039
Age	1.141	.896	.075	1.274	.102
Female [a]	1.489	2.060	.042	.723	.235
Constant	8.919	17.097		.522	.301
r^2	.093				
Adjusted r^2	.066				
N	308				

*p<.05, †one-tailed significance level, [a] reference category = male

Native American substance/drug use OLS regression results are presented in Table 6.8. Significant negative effects on substance/drug use by Native Americans were found for family attachment (B= -1.691, p= .021), school attachment (B= -1.291, p= .000), and self-control (B= -.436, p= .000). Involvement in conventional pursuits produced the now typical positive effect (B= .070, p= .034) on substance/drug use. Significant control variables are age and gender. Age has a positive effect on substance/drug use for Native Americans (B= 2.259, p= .023). Females are less likely to participate in substance/drug use (B= -4.435, p= .045). The combined total effect of the variables in this model explains 24 percent of the variation in substance/drug use by Native Americans (r^2 = .235).

Table 6.8.   OLS Regression, Full Model, Substance/Drug Use,
                    Native American

	B	S.E.	β	t	Sig.†
Parental	-1.033	.672	-.085	-1.536	.063
Family Attach	-1.691*	.826	-.127	-2.047	.021
School Attach	-1.291*	.343	-207	-3.764	.000
Involvement	.070*	.039	.093	1.814	.034
Self-Esteem	.557	.389	.082	1.434	.153
Self-Control	-.436*	.115	-.231	-3.803	.000
Average Grade	-1.785	1.501	-.065	-1.189	.118
Age	2.259*	1.125	.107	2.008	.023
Female[a]	-4.435*	2.597	-.090	-1.708	.045
Constant	34.308	21.089		1.627	.053
r^2	.235				
Adjusted r^2	.212				
N	312				

*p<.05, † one-tailed significance level, [a] reference category = male

CHAPTER 7

Findings for African Americans

INTRODUCTION

This chapter presents the logistic and OLS regression results for African Americans. The first part presents the logistic regression results for the relationships among all of the predictor variables across each measure of delinquency for African Americans. The second part of the chapter presents the results of the OLS regression analyses.

Logistic Regression

The logistic regression results for the African American Sample are displayed in Tables 7.1 through 7.4. The most significant relationships between delinquency and the predictor variables for African Americans are those that involve self-control. Significant inverse relationships exist between self-control and each of the four measures of delinquency – interpersonal delinquency (B=-.075, p<.05), property delinquency (B= -.051, p<.05), vandalism (B= -.031, p<.05) and substance/drug use (B=-.036, p<.05). Significant relationships between interpersonal delinquency and other predictors in Table 7.1 include school attachment (B=-.083, p<.05) and average grade (B=.422, p<.05). The only other predictor besides self-control that is significantly associated with property delinquency in Table 7.2 is involvement in conventional pursuits (B=.010, p<.05), and this relationship is positive.

Table 7.1.   Logistic Regression, Interpersonal Delinquency,
                    African American Sample

	B	S.E.	Wald	Sig. †	Odds-Ratio
Parental	-.078	.096	.665	.208	.925
Family Attach	.125	.121	1.062	.152	1.133
School Attach	-.083*	.050	2.736	.049	.921
Involvement	.003	.006	.305	.291	1.003
Self-Esteem	.052	.049	1.087	.149	1.053
Self-Control	-.075*	.019	16.444	.000	.927
Average Grade	.422*	.243	3.019	.041	1.524
Age	-.035	.167	.044	.417	.966
Female [a]	.101	.395	.066	.399	1.106
Constant	4.281	3.2651	1.733	.099	72.284
Chi-square	26.134				
Chi-square sig.	.000				
df	9				
-2 Log Likelihood	183.594				
Cox & Snell R^2/ Nagelkerke R^2	.15/.21				
N	159				

*$p<.05$, † one-tailed significance level, [a] reference category = male

Significant relationships for vandalism and the predictor variables in Table 7.3 include parental supervision (B=-.193, p<.05), family attachment (B=-.266, p<.05), and average grade (B =-.508, p<.05). In addition, self-esteem produced a positive effect on vandalism (B= .101, p<.05) for African Americans. In Table 7.4 self-control is the only predictor that was significant in relation to substance/drug use (B=-.036, p<.05), for African Americans. A one-unit increase in self-control results in a seven percent decrease in the likelihood of interpersonal delinquency for African Americans. A one-unit increase in self-control results in about a five percent decrease in the likelihood of property delinquency, a three percent decrease in the likelihood of vandalism, and about a four percent decrease in the likelihood of substance/drug use for African Americans.

Table 7.2. Logistic Regression, Property Delinquency, African
American Sample.

	B	S.E.	Wald	Sig.†	Odds-Ratio
Parental	-025	.093	.070	.396	.976
Family Attach	.080	.114	.492	.242	1.083
School Attach	-.024	.048	.248	.309	.976
Involvement	.010*	.006	3.306	.035	1.010
Self-Esteem	.010	.048	.045	.416	1.010
Self-Control	-.051*	.017	9.095	.002	.950
Average Grade	-.132	.231	.326	.284	.876
Age	.035	.159	.049	.412	1.036
Female [a]	-.420	.363	1.205	.136	.657
Constant	2.720	3.153	.744	.194	15.180
Chi-square	20.389				
Chi-square sig.	.016				
df	9				
-2 Log Likelihood	189.037				
Cox &Snell R^2/ Nagelkerke R^2	.13/.17				
N	152				

*$p<.05$, † one-tailed significance level, [a] reference category = male

Table 7.3.Logistic Regression, Vandalism, African American Sample

	B	S.E.	Wald	Sig.	Odds-Ratio
Parental	-.193*	.103	3.487	.031	.824
Family Attach	-.266*	.133	4.021	.023	.766
School Attach	.000	.051	.000	.498	1.000
Involvement	.004	.006	.519	.236	1.004
Self-Esteem	.101*	.059	2.911	.044	1.106
Self-Control	-.031*	.018	3.128	.039	.969
Average Grade	-.508*	.257	3.921	.024	.602
Age	-.092	.184	.250	.309	.912
Female [a]	-.465	.419	1.230	.134	.628
Constant	4.196	3.564	1.386	.120	66.414
Chi-square	21.843				
Chi-square sig.	.009				
df	9				
-2 Log Likelihood	167.616				
Cox & nell R^2/ Nagelkerke R^2	.13/.18				
N	159				

$p<.05$, † one-tailed significance level, [a] reference category = male

The Effects of Race and Family Attachment

A one-unit increase in family attachment results in about a 23 percent decrease in the likelihood of vandalism for African Americans. Grade point average has a negative impact on vandalism for African Americans. A one-unit increase in average grade results in a 40 percent decrease in the likelihood of vandalism. This is an unexpected finding that will be discussed in greater detail in the concluding chapter. No significant gender differences were observed for African Americans.

Table 7.4.   Logistic Regression, Substance/Drug Use, African American Sample

	B	S.E.	Wald	Sig.	Odds-Ratio
Parental	.004	.090	.002	.485	1.004
Family Attach	-.006	.109	.003	.478	.994
School Attach	-.033	.045	.534	.233	.967
Involvement	.002	.005	.127	.361	1.002
Self-Esteem	.052	.049	1.101	.147	1.053
Self-Control	-.036*	.015	5.602	.009	.964
Average Grade	-.196	.226	.752	.193	.822
Age	.260	.160	2.648	.052	1.296
Female [a]	.448	.372	1.450	.114	1.565
Constant	-3.089	3.093	.998	.159	.046
Chi-square	15.324				
Chi-square sig.	.082				
df	9				
-2 Log Likelihood	207.556				
Cox &Snell R^2/ Nagelkerke R^2	.09/.12				
N	165				

*$p<.05$, † one-tailed significance level, [a] reference category = male

OLS Regression
OLS regression analysis results for African Americans are displayed in Tables 7.5 through 7.8. Table 7.5 presents results for interpersonal delinquency. The significant predictors that have an inverse effect on interpersonal delinquency for African Americans are parental supervision (B=-1.369, p= .008) and self-control (B=-.193, p= .019). Interpersonal delinquency is decreased for African Americans by

parental supervision and self-control. School attachment is also in the expected inverse direction but it is not quite significant, and family attachment has absolutely no significance.

Self-esteem has a positive effect (B=.666, p=.012) on interpersonal delinquency for African Americans. No significance was found for any of the control variables. The combined total effect of the variables in this model accounts for approximately thirteen percent of the variance in interpersonal delinquency among African Americans (r^2= .134).

Property delinquency OLS regression results for African Americans are listed in Table 7.6. The predictors that produced a negative effect on property delinquency for African Americans are school attachment (B= -.379, p= .010) and self-control (B= -.101, p= .029). The control variable, gender (female), also had a negative effect (B = -3.114, p= .009). Self-esteem has a positive effect (B= .270, p= .049) on property delinquency for African Americans, as does involvement in conventional pursuits (B=.024, p=.018). The combined total effect of the variables in this model explains 17 percent of the variance in property delinquency among African Americans (r^2 = .17).

Table 7.5. OLS Regression, Full Model, Interpersonal Delinquency, African American

	B	S.E.	β	t	Sig.†
Parental	-1.369*	.559	-.210	-2.451	.008
Family Attach	.507	.682	.065	.743	.229
School Attach	-.440	.283	-.130	1.553	.062
Involvement	.031	.032	.080	.982	.164
Self-Esteem	.666*	.290	.194	2.297	.012
Self-Control	-.193*	.092	-.190	-2.094	.019
Avg. Grade	1.821	1.390	.108	1.310	.096
Age	-1.528	.960	-.124	1.591	.057
Female[a]	1.273	2.275	.045	.560	.289
Constant	39.990	18.626		2.147	.017
r^2	.134				
Adjusted r^2	.082				
N	158				

*p<.05, †one-tailed significance level, [a] reference category = male

Table 7.6.   OLS Regression, Full Model, Property Delinquency
              African American

	B	S.E.	β	t	Sig.†
Parental	-.223	.314	-.061	-.709	.240
Family Attach.	.595	.387	.134	1.537	.064
School Attach.	-.379*	.160	-.199	-2.364	.010
Involvement	.024*	.018	.172	2.117	.018
Self-Esteem	.270*	.162	.140	1.664	.049
Self-Control	-.101*	.053	-.175	-1.918	.029
Avg. Grade	-1.156	.781	-.123	-1.480	.071
Age	-.682	.541	-.098	-1.261	.105
Female[a]	-3.114*	1.294	-.194	-2.406	.009
Constant	27.078	10.526		2.572	.006
r^2	.17				
Adjusted r^2	.11				
N	151				

*p<.05, † one-tailed significance level, [a] reference category = male

Vandalism OLS regression results for African Americans are presented in Table 7.7. Significant negative effects were found for parental supervision (B=-.711, p= .002) and school attachment (B=-.291, p=.009). Although self-control did not produce a significant effect (B=-.063, p=.057) on vandalism for African Americans, it is in the hypothesized inverse direction. Self-esteem has a positive effect (B= 255, p=.020) on vandalism for African Americans. The total combined effect of the variables in this model accounts for 15 percent (r^2 = .15) of the variance in vandalism for African Americans.

Table 7.8 shows the OLS regression results for substance/drug use by African Americans. Significant inverse effects were found for school attachment (B=-.826, p=.002) and self-control (B=-.243, p= .005). A positive relationship was observed between substance/drug use and self-esteem (B=.796, p=.004) for African Americans.

Two control variables are significant, age (B= 1.907, p= .028) and gender/female (B=-4.953, p=.017). An increase in age has a positive effect on substance/drug use. Age contributes to an increase in substance/drug use for African Americans, rather than to the expected reduction. African American females are less likely to engage in substance/drug use than African American males. The total combined effect of the variables in this model accounts for 22 percent (r²= .22) of the variance in substance/drug use for African Americans.

Table 7.7. OLS Regression, Full Model, Vandalism, African American

	B	S.E.	β	t	Sig.†
Parental	-.711*	.238	-.251	-2.985	.002
Family Attach	.216	289	.064	.747	.228
School Attach	-.291*	.120	-.200	-2.423	.009
Involvement	.001	.013	.008	.105	.459
Self-Esteem	.255*	.122	.173	2.087	.020
Self-Control	-.063	.040	-.143	-1.595	.057
Avg. Grade	-.139	.583	-.019	-.239	.406
Age	-.328	.413	-.061	-.794	.214
Female[a]	-.606	.960	-.050	-.631	.265
Constant	18.446	7.977		2,312	.011
r²	.15				
Adjusted r²	.10				
N	158				

*p<.05, † one-tailed significance level, [a] reference category = male

Table 7.8. OLS Regression, Full Model, Substance/Drug Use, African American

	B	S.E.	β	t	Sig.†
Parental	.577	.573	.080	1.005	.158
Family Attach	.632	.687	.074	.920	.180
School Attach	-.826*	.281	-.231	-2.936	.002
Involvement	.003	.033	.007	.097	.462
Self-Esteem	.796*	.298	.208	2.675	.004
Self-Control	-.243*	.093	-.220	-2.600	.005
Avg. Grade	-1.817	1.415	-.098	-1.284	.101
Age	1.907*	.986	.140	1.934	.028
Female[a]	-4.953*	2.315	-.161	-2.139	.017
Constant	-15.577	19.118		-.815	.208
r²	.22				
Adjusted r²	.18				

*p<.05, † one-tailed significance level, [a] reference category = male

CHAPTER 8

Findings for Whites

INTRODUCTION

This chapter presents the logistic and OLS regression results for Whites. The first part of the chapter discusses the logistic regression results. The sample size varies because comparisons are being made across delinquency types. The latter part of the chapter describes the OLS regression results.

Logistic Regression

Logistic regression results for Whites are displayed in Tables 8.1 - 8.4. Significant findings were observed in the relationships between interpersonal delinquency and the following predictors: family attachment (B=-.077,p< .05), self-control (B=-.071, p<.05), average grade (B=-.237, p<.05), and female (B=-.674, p<.05). Significant findings for the predictors' relationships to property delinquency include family attachment (B=-.210, p<.05), involvement in conventional pursuits (B=.006, p<.05), self-control (B=-.050, p<.05), average grade (B=-.220, p<.05) and female (B=-.625, p<.05). Significant findings for vandalism include family attachment (B= -.180, p<.05),school attachment(B=-.049,p<.05), involvement in conventional pursuits (B=.007, p<.05), self-control (B=-.063, p<.05), and female (B= -.742, p<.05). Substance/drug use produced significant findings for self-control (B=-.047, p<.05), family attachment (B=-.140, p<.05), school attachment (B=-.046, p<.05), self-esteem (B=.055, p<.05), average grade (B= -.352, p<.05), and age (B= .208, p<.05).

Table 8.1 displays significant findings for interpersonal delinquency by Whites. A one-unit increase in family attachment decreases the likelihood of interpersonal delinquency by seven percent. A one-unit increase in self-control results in about a seven percent decrease in the likelihood of interpersonal delinquency for Whites. Average grade and gender also decrease the likelihood of interpersonal delinquency for Whites. A one-unit increase in grade point average results in a 21 percent decrease in delinquency, and White females are 49 percent less likely to participate in interpersonal delinquency than White males.

Logistic regression of property delinquency for Whites is shown in Table 8.2. A one-unit increase in family attachment produces a 19 percent decrease in the likelihood of property offenses for Whites. An unexpected positive relationship was produced between involvement in conventional pursuits and property delinquency. A one-unit increase in involvement in conventional pursuits results in a small (less than one percent) increase in the likelihood of property delinquency for Whites. A one-unit increase in self-control results in about a five percent decrease in the likelihood of property delinquency for Whites. A one-unit increase in grade point average produces a 20 percent decrease in the likelihood of property offenses for Whites, and females are 46 percent less likely to commit property offenses than males.

Vandalism results of logistic regression for Whites are presented in Table 8.3. A one-unit increase in family attachment results in a 16 percent decrease in the likelihood of vandalism for Whites. School attachment decreases the likelihood of vandalism among Whites. A one-unit increase in school attachment produces approximately a five percent decrease in the likelihood of vandalism for Whites. Though small, involvement in conventional pursuits has a significant positive effect on vandalism for Whites. A one-unit increase in conventional pursuits corresponds with less than a one percent increase in the likelihood of vandalism. A one-unit increase in self-control generates about a six percent decline in the likelihood of vandalism for Whites. White females are 52 percent less likely to be involved in vandalism than White males.

Table 8.1.   Logistic Regression, Interpersonal Delinquency,
              White Sample

	B	S.E.	Wald	Sig.†	Odds-Ratio
Parental	.033	.048	.465	.248	1.033
Family Attach	-.077*	.044	3.041	.041	.926
School Attach	-.008	.023	.140	.354	.992
Involvement	.003	.003	1.411	.118	1.003
Self-Esteem	.031	.024	1.761	.093	1.032
Self-Control	-.071*	.008	71.959	.000	.932
Avg. Grade	-.237*	.099	5.742	.009	.789
Age	-.045	.073	.372	.271	.956
Female [a]	-.674*	.157	18.508	.000	.510
Constant	4.605	1.439	10.243	.001	100.016
Chi-square	185.795				
Chi-square sig.	.000				
df	9				
-2 Log Likelihood	1044.021				
Cox & Snell R^2/ Nagelkerke R^2	.17/.24				
N	975				

*$p<.05$, † one-tailed significance level, [a] reference category = male

Table 8.4 presents the logistic regression for substance/drug use by Whites. A one-unit increase in family attachment results in a 13 percent decline in the likelihood of substance/drug use by Whites. A negative relationship exists between school attachment and substance/drug use for Whites. A one-unit increase in school attachment produces a four percent decrease in the likelihood of substance/drug use. A positive relationship was observed for self-esteem and substance/drug use. A one-unit increase in self-esteem generates a 6 percent increase in substance/drug use by Whites. A one-unit increase in self-control produces a 4 percent decrease in the likelihood of substance/drug use for Whites. A one-unit increase in grade point average produces a 30 percent decrease in the likelihood substance/drug use by Whites.

Table 8.2.   Logistic Regression, Property Delinquency, White

	B	S.E.	Wald	Sig.†	Odds-Ratio
Parental	-.058	.047	1.568	.105	.943
Family Attach	-.210*	.042	24.623	.000	.810
School Attach	-.009	.022	.177	.337	.991
Involvement	.006*	.002	6.111	.007	1.006
Self-Esteem	.040*	.023	3.083	.040	1.041
Self-Control	-.050*	.008	41.896	.000	.952
Avg. Grade	-.220*	.096	5.285	.011	.803
Age	-.095	.071	1.788	.091	.909
Female [a]	-.625*	.152	17.009	.000	.535
Constant	5.616	1.392	16.273	.000	274.862
Chi-square	173.124				
Chi-square sig.	.000				
df	9				
-2 Log Likelihood	1115.517				
Cox & Snell R²/ Nagelkerke R²	.17/.23				
N	947				

*p<.05, † one-tailed significance level, [a] reference category = male

Table 8.3.   Logistic Regression, Vandalism, White Sample

	B	S.E.	Wald	Sig.†	Odds-Ratio
Parental	-.053	.049	1.163	.141	.949
Family Attach	-.180*	.046	15.640	.000	.835
School Attach	-.049*	.023	4.692	.015	.952
Involvement	.007*	.003	5.944	.008	1.007
Self-Esteem	-.009	.023	.158	.346	.991
Self-Control	-.063*	.008	55.684	.000	.939
Avg. Grade	.058	.101	.331	.283	1.060
Age	-.063	.076	.682	.205	.939
Female [a]	-.742*	.162	20.956	.000	.476
Constant	6.279	1.499	17.560	.000	533.511
Chi-square	190.501				
Chi-square sig.	.000				
df	9				
-2 Log Likelihood	995.784				
Cox &Snell R²/ Nagelkerke R²	.18/.25				
N	967				

*p<.05, † one-tailed significance level, [a] reference category = male

Table 8.4.   Logistic Regression, Substance/Drug Use, White Sample

	B	S.E.	Wald	Sig.†	Odds-Ratio
Parental	-040	.046	.760	.192	.961
Family Attach	-.140*	.041	11.765	.001	.869
School Attach	-.046*	.022	4.444	.018	.955
Involvement	.004	.002	2.559	.055	1.004
Self-Esteem	.055*	.022	6.245	.006	1.057
Self-control	-.047*	.007	40.310	.000	.954
Avg. Grade	-.352*	.095	13.612	.000	.703
Age	.208*	.072	8.456	.002	1.232
Female	.067	.149	.201	.327	1.069
Constant	1.109	1.360	.664	.208	3.030
Chi-square	163.179				
Chi-square sig.	.000				
df	9				
Cox & Snell R^2/ Nagelkerke R^2	.15/.21				
N	985				

*$p<.05$, † one-tailed significance level, [a] reference category = male

OLS Regression

Tables 8.5 through 8.8 present OLS regression findings for Whites. Interpersonal delinquency significant findings are shown in Table 8.5. The only predictor that produced a significant inverse effect on interpersonal delinquency for Whites is self-control (B=-.075, p= .000). Two of the control variables are significant in the expected direction, average grade (B=-.385, p= .003) and gender (B= -1.033, p= .000). An increase in self-control decreases interpersonal delinquency for Whites. An increase in average grade also reduces interpersonal delinquency for Whites. Being a White female decreases involvement in interpersonal delinquency. The combined total effects of the variables in this model account for 12 percent (r^2 =.12) of the variance in interpersonal delinquency for Whites.

Table 8.5.   OLS Regression, Full Model, Interpersonal Delinquency, White

	B	S.E.	β	t	Sig.†
Parental	.018	.067	.008	.263	.397
Family Attach	-.070	.061	-.040	-1.140	.128
School Attach	.026	.032	.029	.823	.206
Involvement	.008*	.004	.069	2.215	.014
Self-Esteem	.003	.033	.003	.092	.464
Self-Control	-.075*	.011	-.254	-6.961	.000
Avg. Grade	-.385*	.139	-.094	-2.760	.003
Age	-.009	.105	-.003	-.088	.465
Female[a]	-1.033*	221	-.146	-4.667	.000
Constant	6.979	2.006		3.479	.001
r^2	.12				
Adjusted r^2	.11				
N	974				

*$p<.05$, † one-tailed significance level, [a] reference category = male

OLS regression property delinquency results for Whites are displayed in Table 8.6. Significant negative effects were found for parental supervision (B=-.493, p= .001), family attachment (B=-.356, p= .005), and self-control (B=-.121, p= .000). Gender (female) is the only control variable that is significant (B=-2.883, p= .000). An increase in parental supervision decreases property delinquency for Whites by .493. An increase in family attachment results in a .356 decrease in property delinquency, and an increase in self-control generates a .121 decrease in property delinquency for Whites. White females are less likely to engage in property delinquency than are White males. The combined total effects of the variables in this model explain 13 percent of the variance in property delinquency for Whites ($r^2 = .13$).

OLS regression results for vandalism by Whites are shown in Table 8.7. The predictors that produced significant negative effects are family attachment (B=-.242, p=.005), school attachment (B=-.080, p= .046), and self-control (B=-.079, p= .000). Gender (female), a control variable, is also significant (B=-.922, p= .003). These findings indicate that there is an inverse relationship between vandalism and the following predictors: family attachment, school attachment, and self-control for Whites. White females are less likely to engage in vandalism than are White males. The total effect of the variables in this model explains nine percent of the variance in vandalism for Whites ($r^2 = .09$).

Table 8.6.   OLS Regression, Full Model, Property Delinquency, White

	B	S.E.	β	t	Sig.†
Parental	-.493*	.150	-.103	-3.282	.001
Family Attach	-.356*	.135	-.092	-2.632	.005
School Attach	-.041	.070	-.021	-.594	.277
Involvement	.004	.088	.015	.479	.316
Self-Esteem	.077	.073	.036	1.056	.146
Self-Control	-.121*	.024	-.188	-5.123	.000
Avg. Grade	-.468	.307	-.052	-1.526	.064
Age	.043	.230	.006	.188	.426
Female[a]	-2.883*	.487	-.187	-5.926	.000
Constant	17.912	4.418		4.055	.000
r^2	.133				
Adjusted r^2	.124				
N	946				

*p<.05, † one-tailed significance level, [a] reference category = male

Table 8.8 lists the OLS regression results for substance/drug use by Whites. This is the only analysis in which all of the social bonding predictors are significant, even though involvement in conventional pursuits is in the opposite direction. In addition, self-control has an inverse relationship (B=-.307, p=.000) with substance/drug use for Whites. Two control variables were significant – average grade produced an inverse effect (B=-2.811, p= .001), and age has a positive effect (B= 1.552, p= .006).

Table 8.7.   OLS Regression, Full Model, Vandalism, White

	B	S.E.	β	t	Sig.†
Parental	-.146	.102	-.046	-1.441	.075
Family Attach	-.242*	.092	-.093	-2.618	.005
School Attach	-.080*	.047	-.061	-1.693	.046
Involvement	.004	.005	.022	.899	.243
Self-Esteem	.005	.049	.004	.108	.457
Self-Control	-.079*	.016	-.185	-4.932	.000
Avg. Grade	.087	.210	.014	.413	.340
Age.	.158	.157	.032	1.007	.157
Female[a]	-.922*	.332	-.089	-2.778	.003
Constant	7.745	3.024		2.561	.006
r^2	.09				
Adjusted r^2	.08				
N	966				

*p<.05, † one-tailed significance level, [a] reference category = male

The social bonding predictors that have an inverse effect on substance/drug use for Whites include parental supervision (B= -2.811, p=.007), family attachment (B= -.777, p= .015), and school attachment (B= -.840, p =.000). Parental supervision decreases substance/drug use by 2.811; an increase in family attachment decreases substance/drug use by .777, and an increase in school attachment decreases substance/drug use by .840 for Whites. Involvement in conventional pursuits has a positive effect on substance/drug use for Whites (B= .025, p= .014). An increase in grades reduces substance/drug use but an increase in age increases substance/drug use for Whites. The total effects of the variables in this model explain 16 percent of the variance in substance/drug use by Whites (r^2 = .16).

Table 8.8.   OLS Regression, Full Model, Substance/Drug Use, White

	B	S.E.	β	t	Sig.†
Parental	-2.811*	.607	.077	2.557	.007
Family Attach	-.777*	.356	-.074	-2.180	.015
School Attach	-.840*	.184	-.156	-4.569	.000
Involvement	.025*	.021	.067	2.203	.014
Self-Esteem	-.036	.188	-.006	-.189	.425
Self-Control	-.307*	.062	-.176	-4.979	.000
Avg. Grade	-2.811*	.807	-.115	-3.481	.001
Age	1.552*	.607	.007	2.557	.006
Female[a]	-1.752	1.280	-.042	-1.368	.086
Constant	42.264	11.609		3.640	.000
r^2	.16				
Adjusted r^2	.16				
N	984				

*p<.05, † one-tailed significance level, [a] reference category = male

CHAPTER 9

Summary of Racial Group Findings

INTRODUCTION

This chapter summarizes the three preceding race specific chapters. First a summary of the findings for each racial group is presented. Next, a diagram of the significant logistic regression results by race provides a visual summary of the results. This is followed by a summary of the OLS regression results for each racial group with a visual display of those results.

Logistic Regression

In summary, the predictor variable that has the most consistent significant impact on the delinquency indicators is self-control. The impact of self-control significantly decreases the likelihood of delinquency across racial groups. Table 9.1 presents a summary of the logistic regression relationships that were found to be significant. An inverse relationship is observed between the delinquency measure and self-control designated by a negative sign (–). Self-control has the most consistent negative effect on each of the delinquency measures. Family attachment is the social bonding indicator that has the most significant impact on delinquency. Interpersonal delinquency, property delinquency and substance/drug use are decreased by strong family attachment for Native Americans and Whites but not for African Americans. Family attachment does decrease vandalism for African Americans, as well as for Whites but not for Native Americans.

The effect of parental supervision on delinquency is not as strong as family attachment. Property delinquency and vandalism are reduced among Native Americans for those individuals from families who had parental supervision. If Native Americans had parental supervision,

93

were attached to their family or were involved in conventional pursuits, they were less likely to use substances/drugs. In fact, this is the only relationship where involvement in conventional pursuits actually decreased the likelihood of delinquency. Vandalism is the only delinquency indicator that is reduced by parental supervision for African Americans. School attachment is significant only for African Americans in reducing interpersonal delinquency and for Whites in the reduction of vandalism and substance/drug use. It has no effect on delinquency for Native Americans.

Self-esteem did not have the predicted impact on delinquency. All of the significant relationships were found to be positive, indicating that self-esteem increases the likelihood of delinquency, specifically property and substance/drug use for Whites and substance/drug use for Native Americans, as well as vandalism for African Americans. Consequently, those Native Americans and Whites with high self-esteem have a greater likelihood of using substances/drugs. Whites with high self-esteem also have a greater likelihood of participating in property delinquency and African Americans with high self-esteem are more likely to participate in vandalism.

The impacts of grades, age and gender on delinquency were not as strong as expected. Grades had the most significant impact on interpersonal, property, and substance/drug delinquency for Whites. African Americans who make good grades are less likely to participate in vandalism but more likely to participate in interpersonal delinquency. However, a strong significant inverse effect was observed between average grade and vandalism for African Americans. An increase in average grades results in a 40 percent decrease in the likelihood of vandalism for African Americans. There was no significant impact of grades on delinquency for Native Americans. Age only affects substance/drug use for African Americans and Whites by increasing the likelihood of use as age increases.

Table 9.1. Summary of Significant Logistic Regression Relationships for Total Sample and by Race

Predictor	Interpersonal				Property				Vandalism				Substance/Drug Use			
	Total	N.A	A.A	Wh.	Total	N.A	A.A	Wh.	Total	N.A	A.A	Wh.	Total	N.A	A.A	Wh.
Parental Super.	–			–		–			–	–	–		–	–		–
Family Attach.		–		–		–	–	–	–		–	–	–	–		–
School Attach.			–									–	–			
Involvement	+				+	+	+	+	+			+		–		
Self-Esteem	+					–	+	+	–		+	–	+	+	+	+
Self-Control		–		–	–		–	–		–	–		–	–	–	
Avg. Grade	–		+	–	–			–					–	–	+	
Age												–	+	+	+	+
Gender	–	–		–	–			–	–					+		+

(N.A. - Native American, A.A. - African American, Wh - White)

Native American and White females are less likely than are their male counterparts to participate in interpersonal delinquency and vandalism. White females are also less likely to participate in property delinquency than are their male counterparts. No significant gender effects were observed for African Americans.

OLS Regression

Table 9.2 presents a summary of the OLS regression significant full model results for the predictor and control variables across each of the four delinquency measures for each ethnic group. The primary predictors are social bonding, self-esteem and self-control. The control variables are average grade, age, and gender.

Social Bonding

Four social bonding measures were examined: parental supervision, school attachment, family attachment, and involvement in conventional pursuits. Of the four indicators that had negative effects on delinquency, parental supervision had the weakest effect. It works more for African Americans and Whites than it does for Native Americans. Parental supervision decreases interpersonal delinquency and vandalism for African Americans and it decreases property delinquency and substance/drug use for Whites, but it has no effect on delinquency for Native Americans. Involvement in conventional pursuits, the fourth measure of social bonding, does not decrease delinquency; instead it has a positive effect on delinquency. It increases interpersonal delinquency and substance/drug use for Whites and increases property delinquency for African Americans. Involvement in conventional pursuits also increases property delinquency, vandalism and substance/drug use for Native Americans.

Table 9.2. Summary of OLS Regression Significant Full Model Results

Predictor	Interpersonal Delinquency			Property Delinquency			Vandalism Delinquency			Substance/drug Delinquency		
	N.A.	A.A.	Wh.	N.A.	A.A.	Wh.	N.A.	A.A.	Wh.	N.A.	A.A.	Wh.
Parental Supervision		–						–				–
Family Attach.				–	–						–	–
School Attach.			+	+	+					+		+
Involvement		+		+	+		+				+	
Self-Esteem					+			+			+	
Self-Control	–	–	–	–	–	–	–		–	–	–	–
Average Grade							–			+	+	+
Age										–	–	+
Female [a]	–		–	–	–	–			–		–	–

[a] reference category = male

Self-Esteem

No inverse effects were observed for self-esteem in reference to any of the delinquency measures. African American is the only ethnic group that experienced increased delinquency as self-esteem increased. This positive effect occurred across each type of delinquency.

Self-Control

The presence of self-control decreases involvement in delinquency across race, regardless of the type of delinquency. Self-control is the predictor that has the most consistent impact on delinquency. The findings are consistent with expectations.

Control Variables

The effect of average grade on delinquency was more significant for Whites. Interpersonal delinquency and substance/drug use were significantly impacted by age for Whites. Vandalism was decreased for Native Americans as a result of grades, but no effect was found for African Americans. No significant effects were observed for age and interpersonal delinquency, property delinquency or vandalism. An increase in substance/drug use was observed in relation to age. Females were less likely to be delinquents compared to males. However, this applies more to Whites and Native Americans than African Americans. White females are less likely to commit interpersonal, property and vandalism delinquency than White males. Native American females are less likely to participate in interpersonal, property and substance/drug use delinquency than Native American males. African American females are less likely to participate in property delinquency and substance/drug use than African American males.

CHAPTER 10

Findings for Social Bonding, Self-Esteem and Self-Control as Dependent Variables

Social bonding was examined as a dependent variable to determine how the significance and strength of the associations compare to the findings produced by social bonding as an independent variable. Self-esteem was examined as a dependent variable to determine if a positive relationship exists between delinquency and self-esteem in which high delinquency increases self-esteem. Self-control was used as a dependent variable primarily to examine the reciprocal effects of social bonding.

Table 10.1 presents the OLS regression results for social bonding and self-control as the dependent variable. Four social bonding measures are used – parental supervision, school attachment, family attachment and involvement in conventional pursuits. Three of the social bonding measures produced significant positive effects. The significant findings include school attachment (B= .749, p=.000), family attachment (B= 2.137, p=.000), and involvement in conventional pursuits (B= .031, p=.001). These findings indicate that an increase in social bonding contributes to an increase in self-control. School attachment increases self-control by .75, family attachment increases self-control by 2.137, and involvement in conventional pursuits contributes to a .031 percent increase in self-control. Although insignificant, an unexpected negative relationship was observed between parental supervision and self-control. The combined total effects of the variables in this model explain 23 percent of the variance in self-control ($r^2 = .23$).

Table 10.1.   OLS Regression of Social Bonding and Self-Control
                 (Dependent Variable)

	B	S.E.	β	t	Sig.†
Parental Super.	-.131	.163	-.019	-.807	.210
Family Attach.	2.137*	.156	.330	13.727	.000
School Attach.	.749*	.077	.238	9.749	.000
Involvement	.031*	.009	.077	3.342	.001
Constant	42.031	2.026		20.750	.000
r^2	.23				
Adjusted r^2	.22				
N	1501				

*p<.05, † one-tailed significance level

OLS regression results of social bonding and self-esteem as a dependent variable are shown in Table 10.2. A significant positive effect is produced for each of the four social bonding measures and self-esteem. The significant findings include parental supervision (B= .329, p=.000), school attachment (B=.110, p=.000), family attachment (B=.441, p=.000), and involvement in conventional pursuits (B=.007, p=.006). An increase in social bonding contributes to an increase in self-esteem. An increase in parental supervision increases self-esteem by .329, an increase in school attachment increases self-esteem by .110, an increase in family attachment increases self-esteem by .441, and an increase in involvement in conventional pursuits increases self-esteem by .007 percent.

Table 10.2.   OLS Regression of Social Bonding and Self-Esteem
                 (Dependent Variable)

	B	S.E.	β	t	Sig.†
Parental Super.	.329*	.050	.159	6.614	.000
Family Attach.	.441*	.047	.232	9.320	.000
School Attach.	.110*	.023	.120	4.756	.000
Involvement	.007*	.003	.061	2.542	.006
Constant	15.801	.624		25.331	.000
r^2	.136				
Adjusted r^2	.134				
N	1557				

*p<.05, † one-tailed significance level

Social bonding as measured by parental supervision, school attachment, family attachment and involvement in conventional pursuits explains approximately 14 percent of the variation in self-esteem ($r^2 = .136$).

Table 10.3. lists the OLS regression results for self-esteem and self-control as a dependent variable. The results indicate that a positive relationship does exist between self-esteem and self-control. An increase in self-esteem contributes to an increase in self-control. Though significant, only a small amount of the variance in self-control, about five percent, can be explained by self-esteem ($r^2 = .047$).

Table 10.3. OLS Regression of Self-Esteem and Self-Control (Dependent Variable)

	B	S.E.	β	t	Sig.†
Self-Esteem	.735*	.083	.216	8.836	.000
Constant	45.976	1.936		23.746	.000
df	1				
r^2	.047				
Adjusted r^2	.046				
N	1596				

*p<.05, †one-tailed significance level

Summary of Findings for Self-Esteem as Dependent Variable

Does self-esteem vary by delinquency type and race, and does delinquency impact self-esteem positively?   These questions are examined in this section because prior research, as well as findings in the present study, raises those questions (see Figure 1). Researchers do not agree on the relationship between self-esteem and delinquency. Some argue that high self-esteem decreases delinquency (Reckless, 1961; Kaplan, 1982) while others suggest that it is high delinquency that increases self-esteem (McCarthy and Hoge, 1984; Wells, 1989; Rosenberg et al., 1989). Analyzing self-esteem as a dependent variable addresses the latter part of this debate and will provide more information on what motivates people to participate in delinquency. Table 10.4 presents a summary of OLS regression findings with self-esteem as the dependent variable. Twenty data runs listed in Appendix

C were used to generate this summary. The data were analyzed using the full sample and by race. Each measure of delinquency (interpersonal, property, vandalism and substance/drug use) was entered separately and together.

Interpersonal delinquency was observed to have a positive relationship with self-esteem for the total sample as well as for African Americans. The relationship between interpersonal delinquency and self-esteem is not significant for Native Americans or Whites.

The relationship between property delinquency and self-esteem is also positive for the total sample and African Americans but is not significant for Native Americans or Whites. The same relationship is observed between vandalism and self-esteem. It is positive for the total sample and not significant for Native Americans or Whites. The relationship between substance/drug use and self-esteem is positive only for African Americans but not the total sample or Native Americans or Whites.

When all four measures are entered into the model, the significance of the impact on self-esteem is not as strong. Interpersonal delinquency has a positive relationship with self-esteem only for the total sample. No delinquency measures show significance in their relationship with self-esteem for Native Americans or Whites. However, the relationship between substance/drug use and self-esteem remains significantly positive for African Americans.

Other significant findings in relation to the predictors and self-esteem include the following:

1. Parental supervision is the only predictor that has a significant positive impact on self-esteem across each measure of delinquency for each race.
2. Self-control has a positive effect on self-esteem across each measure of delinquency for only African Americans.
3. Family attachment has a positive effect on self-esteem across each delinquency measure for Native Americans and Whites. The relationship between family attachment and self-esteem is positive across interpersonal delinquency and substance/drug use, but not property delinquency or vandalism for African Americans.
4. School attachment has a positive effect on self-esteem across all delinquency measures for Whites but not Native Americans or African Americans.

5. Involvement in conventional pursuits has a significantly positive impact on self-esteem for Whites when interpersonal delinquency or property delinquency is entered separately into the model and when all four measures are entered at the same time.

6. No significance was observed in the relationship between involvement in conventional pursuits and self-esteem when the delinquency measures are entered into the model for Native Americans. A positive relationship exists for vandalism and substance/drug use by African Americans.

7. Average grade and age have significant impacts on self-esteem across all delinquency measure for Native Americans and Whites. However, neither grades nor age significantly impact self-esteem for African Americans.

8. African American females have higher self-esteem than African American males, and White males have higher self-esteem than White females, across each measure of delinquency. In terms of interpersonal delinquency, Native American females have more self-esteem than Native American males, but in relation to vandalism, Native American females have lower self-esteem than Native American males.

Table 10.4. Summary of OLS Regression Significant Results, Self-Esteem – Dependent Variable

PREDICTORS	Total Sample					Native American					African American					White				
	I	P	V	S	D	I	P	V	S	D	I	P	V	S	D	I	P	V	S	D
Parental	+	+	+	+	+	+	+	+	+	+	+	+	+	+	+	+	+	+	+	+
Family	+	+	+	+	+	+	+	+	+	+	+	0	0	0	0	+	+	+	+	+
School	+	+	+	+	+	0	0	0	0	0	0	0	0	0	0	+	+	+	+	+
Involvement	+	+	+	0	+	0	0	0	0	0	0	+	+	+	0	+	+	0	0	+
Self-control	0	0	0	0	+	0	0	0	0	0	+	+	+	+	+	0	0	0	0	0
Average grade	+	+	+	+	+	+	+	+	+	+	0	0	0	0	0	+	+	+	+	+
Age	+	+	+	+	+	+	+	+	+	+	+	+	+	+	+	+	+	+	+	+
Female [a]	-	-	-	-	-	+	0	-	0	0	+				0	-	-	-	-	-
Interpersonal	+	+			+	+	0			0	+	+			+	0	-	-	-	0
Property		+	0		0		0	0		0		+	0		0		0	0		0
Vandalism			0	0	0			0	0	0			0	0	0			0	0	0
Substance/drug			0	0	0			0	0	0			+	+	+			0	0	0

[a] reference category = male, (I - Interpersonal, P- Property, V- Vandalism, S-Substance/drug , D- All four delinquency measures), (+) - positive significance, (–) - negative significance, 0 – not significant

CHAPTER 11

Summary and Conclusions

Hirschi's social bonding theory is central to this research because it examines behavior development and the early relationship between children and parents. The early bonding between parent and child is believed to be very crucial to the development of behavior and other traits, specifically self-control. Gottfredson and Hirschi developed self-control theory separately from social bonding theory, but this research emphasizes the link between them. It is proposed that the two theories are complementary of each other. The perspective used in this study is that they operate on a continuum. If effective social bonding takes place during the early stages of a child's development, it is more likely to result in stronger self-control as an adult. As the child ages, self-control develops out of a desire to first please parents and it continues to develop as the child becomes an adult who desires to become a viable, contributing member of society. Low self-control is more likely to develop when the desired bonding does not take place, and this increases the risk of delinquency. A lack of social bonding may also explain why delinquency may increase self-esteem. Proponents of strain theory suggest that general strain leads to weakened bonds to society and this in turn contributes to delinquency (Paternoster and Mazerolle, 1994; Brezina, 1996). However, the assumption of this research is that the weakened bonds to significant others at an early age precede strain. Consequently, when bonding to parents does not take place at an early age, the likelihood of participation in delinquency increases. Participation in delinquency can then lead to an increase in self-esteem.

It is important to understand that self-esteem does not necessarily develop from only positive socially approved circumstances. It can develop from activities and circumstances that do not have society's approval. The activities may be without merit, and they may be egotistical or self-indulging. Therefore, this type of self-esteem is not sanctioned and is indicative of low self-control and lack of conscience.

Brezina (2000) emphasizes "the problem-solving framework" as an explanation for delinquency. This framework posits that delinquency may be a form of self-regulation. According to Brezina, delinquency that goes unpunished may alleviate emotional stress experienced by adolescents as they deal with day-to-day events. Adolescents are more susceptible to the negative events in their life, which they perceive to be greater than those of children or adults. Delinquent acts such as truancy and running away from home are used as a means of escape from environments where stress is produced. Adolescents may use delinquent behavior, such as alcohol/drug use, to counteract depression and despair (Wood et al., 1997). Brezina summarizes factors, outlined in relevant literature, that have been found to determine whether adolescents choose delinquent rather than conventional problem solving methods. These factors include: (1) the availability of conventional problem-solving alternatives, (2) the outcome expectancies attached to delinquent coping techniques, and (3) the efficacy of delinquent adaptations (Brezina, 2000). Brezina further argues that the choice of conventional problem solving strategies is related to self-control, which requires a measure of restraint or impulse control.

The hypothesized relationships in this study include the belief that high scores on social bonding will result in high scores on self-esteem, high scores on self-control, and low scores on delinquency. Initial bivariate findings indicated a strong correlation between self-control and delinquency. The association between social bonding and delinquency was found to be statistically significant. The strongest correlations using Pearson's r analysis are between family attachment and the delinquency measures, followed by school attachment and parental supervision, which had the least significant associations. When social bonding is measured by family attachment and school attachment it is moderately correlated with self-esteem. Social bonding and self-control are also significantly associated. All of the social bonding measures are significantly associated with self-control. The initial bivariate analysis overwhelmingly supported additional analyses of the hypothesized relationships.

Logistic regression and OLS analyses allowed for a multifaceted examination of the data that either fully or partially supported the hypothesized relationships.

Research Questions and Hypotheses

I. What is the role of social bonding in the development of delinquency?

H1. Social bonding is negatively related to delinquency.

H2. Social bonding is positively related to self-control.

H3. Social bonding is positively related to self-esteem.

H4. The effect of social bonding on delinquency is mediated by self-esteem.

II. How does self-control impact delinquency, self-esteem and social bonding?

H5. Self-control is negatively related to delinquency.

H6. The impact of social bonding on delinquency is mediated by self-control.

H7. Self-control is positively related to self-esteem.

III. What is the nature of the impact of self-esteem on delinquency?

H8. Net of other predictors, self-esteem has a negative impact on delinquency.

IV. What role does race place in the association between social bonding, self-control, self-esteem and delinquency?

H9. The relative impacts of social bonding, self-control and self-esteem on delinquency will vary by race.

H10. The relative impacts of social bonding, self-control and delinquency on self-esteem will vary by race.

V. What is the impact of delinquency on self-esteem?

H11. Net of other predictors, delinquency has a positive impact on self-esteem.

Table 11.1 is a summary of the findings. The relevant logistic regression and OLS findings can also be viewed in Tables 5.5, 9.1 and 9.2.

H₁. Social bonding is negatively related to delinquency.

This hypothesis is partially supported by logistic regression and OLS regression. . The measures of social bonding used in this study are parental supervision, family attachment, school attachment and involvement in conventional pursuits.

Logistic regression findings indicate that family attachment is the social bonding indicator with the greatest effect on delinquency. It decreased the likelihood of interpersonal delinquency, property delinquency and substance/drug use for Native Americans and Whites. It also decreased the likelihood of vandalism for African Americans, as well as for Whites. Parental supervision decreased property delinquency and vandalism for Native Americans, vandalism for African Americans, but it had no effect on delinquency for Whites. School attachment decreased the likelihood of interpersonal delinquency for both African Americans and Whites but it had no effect on delinquency for Native Americans. Involvement in conventional pursuits did not produce the predicted negative effects. There was only one relationship that was in the predicted direction, and that is the reduction of substance/drug use by Native Americans who were involved in conventional pursuits.

OLS regression results show an inverse relationship between interpersonal delinquency and social bonding in the form of parental supervision, for African Americans but not for Native Americans or Whites. OLS regression results indicate that school attachment is the social bonding indicator with the strongest effect on delinquency. School attachment decreased the likelihood of property delinquency for both Native Americans and African Americans; it decreased vandalism for African Americans and Whites; and it decreased substance/drug use for all three ethnic groups. Family attachment has the next strongest effect. It decreased the likelihood of property delinquency for Native Americans and Whites; it decreased vandalism for Whites; and it decreased substance/drug use for Native Americans and Whites. Parental supervision decreases the likelihood of property delinquency for Whites, vandalism for African Americans, and substance/drug use for Whites. According to OLS regression results, parental supervision has no effect on the delinquency of Native Americans.

H_2. Social bonding is positively related to self-control.

Hypothesis 2 is partially supported. OLS regression results, which identify self-control as the dependent variable and the social bonding indicators as the predictors, produced significant positive effects for three of the social bonding measures. Parental supervision was not significant. The other three measures of social bonding – family attachment, school attachment and involvement in conventional pursuits – were positively associated with self-control, as hypothesized.

H₃. Social bonding is positively related to self-esteem.

OLS regression results for this hypothesis, which identifies self-esteem as the dependent variable and the social bonding indicators as predictors, support this hypothesis. All of the social bonding measures – parental supervision, family attachment, school attachment and involvement in conventional pursuits – generated significant, positive results. Thus, an increase in social bonding produces an increase in self-esteem.

H₄. The effect of social bonding on delinquency is mediated by self-esteem.

This hypothesis is not supported. A summary of the results in Table 5.5 reveals that no changes in findings were observed for social bonding as a result of adding self-esteem to the model. The effect of social bonding on delinquency was only partially mediated by self-esteem in reference to substance/drug use. The relationship is positive and no additional effect on the model is observed by the addition of self-esteem.

H₅. Self-control is negatively related to delinquency.

Hypothesis 5 is supported by both logistic and OLS regression. Logistic regression produced significant results for self-control that are negatively related to all four measures of delinquency for each of the three ethnic groups. OLS regression supported the negative effects of self-control on all forms of delinquency for each race except for vandalism by African Americans.

H₆. The impact of social bonding on delinquency is mediated by self-control.

Partial support was found for this hypothesis. Logistic regression models in Table 5.5 show the results of adding social bonding in column two. School attachment, which generated the strongest effect in the OLS regression, fails to maintain that effect when self-control is added, and the significant negative effect on property delinquency is lost. The effect of school attachment on vandalism is also diminished when self-control is added. Adding self-control to the model generated a significant inverse effect between substance/drug use and parental supervision.

H₇. Self-control is positively related to self-esteem.

This hypothesis is supported. OLS regression results which list self-control as the dependent variable and self-esteem as the predictor produced a significant positive effect.

H₈. Net of other predictors, self-esteem has a negative impact on delinquency.

Hypothesis 8 is not supported by either logistic regression or OLS regression. No negative effects on delinquency were produced by self-esteem. Logistic regression produced a positive relationship between self-esteem and property delinquency for Whites; a positive relationship between self-esteem and vandalism for African-Americans; and a positive relationship between self-esteem and substance/drug use for Native Americans and Whites. The results of OLS regression for African Americans were all significantly positive for the relationships between self-esteem and each measure of delinquency. The relationship between self-esteem and delinquency, when self-esteem is the independent variable, is significant in the total sample only for interpersonal delinquency and that relationship is positive. No significance was observed for Native Americans or Whites. Significance was observed for African Americans, but that significance is positive.

H₉. The relative impacts of social bonding, self-control and self-esteem on delinquency will vary by race.

Hypothesis 9 is supported. Race variations were found in the effects of the primary predictors (social bonding, self-control and self-esteem) on delinquency. The least variation was observed for self-control. Logistic regressions of the full model did not support race variation for self-control and the delinquency measures. However, variations were observed in OLS regression because self-control does not have a significant effect on vandalism for African Americans. Social bonding had the greatest effect on delinquency for Native Americans. Property delinquency and substance/drug use were decreased for Native Americans by parental supervision and family attachment. Vandalism was decreased by parental supervision for Native Americans. African Americans also experienced a decrease in vandalism as a result of parental supervision and family attachment. Family attachment decreased each type of delinquency for Whites. Self-esteem was not significant in decreasing delinquency for either race. The logistic regression results in Table 5.5 indicate more interpersonal delinquency for Native Americans when compared to Whites; more property delinquency for African Americans when compared to Whites; and less substance/drug use for African Americans when compared to Whites.

OLS regression race-specific results reveal a greater effect of the predictors on delinquency for Whites than for Native Americans or African Americans. School attachment produced negative effects on property delinquency, vandalism and substance/drug use for African Americans. Inverse relationships were observed between school attachment and property delinquency, as well as between school attachment and substance/drug use, for Native Americans. School attachment generated a decrease in vandalism and in substance/drug use for Whites. Family attachment produced negative effects on property delinquency and substance/drug use for Native Americans and Whites, as well as vandalism for Whites, but no effects were observed for African Americans. Self-esteem effects were positive for African Americans across each type of delinquency. The effects of self-control are not significant for vandalism by African Americans.

H_{10}. The relative impacts of social bonding, self-control and delinquency on self-esteem will vary by race.
This hypothesis is supported by the OLS regression findings. The impact of social bonding on self-esteem does vary by race. Three of the four measures of social bonding (school attachment, family attachment and involvement in convenient pursuits), had some impact on self-esteem that varied by racial group. School attachment had a positive effect on all measures of delinquency for the total sample. However, significance was observed for only Whites when comparing the results for the racial groups. School attachment has a positive effect on self-esteem for Whites.

The relationship between family attachment and self-esteem is significant across all delinquency measures for the total sample. Family attachment has a positive effect on self-esteem for the total sample. That relationship is also positive for Native Americans and Whites in relationship to each delinquency measure. Positive significance was also observed in the relationship between family attachment and self-esteem as they impact interpersonal delinquency and substance/drug use for African Americans, but no significance was observed for property delinquency and vandalism.

The relationship between involvement in conventional pursuits and self-esteem is positively significant for each measure of delinquency in the total sample, except substance/drug use. No significance was observed for Native Americans. Positive significance was observed for vandalism and substance/drug use for African Americans, and interpersonal delinquency and property delinquency for Whites.

Parental supervision had the strongest impact on self-esteem, which was positive, and it did not vary by race. The significance of parental supervision in relation to self- esteem is consistently positive across each racial group and each measure of delinquency.

The relationship between self-control and self-esteem is significant only for African Americans. The impact of self-control on self-esteem affects each measure of delinquency positively for African Americans. No significance is observed for Native Americans or Whites.

The relative impact of delinquency on self-esteem does vary by race. No significance was observed for Native Americans or Whites, but significance was observed for African Americans.

H_{11}. Net of other predictors, delinquency has a positive impact on self-esteem.

Partial support for this hypothesis was observed. A positive effect of delinquency on self-esteem was observed for the total sample for each delinquency measure except substance/drug use. This effect was observed for each delinquency measure when it was entered separately. This impact did not hold when all delinquency measures were entered into the model, except for interpersonal delinquency. African American is the only racial group for which a significant positive relationship was observed between delinquency and self-esteem.

The majority of the hypothesized relationships were supported by the analyses. Five of the eleven hypotheses were fully supported, four of the hypotheses were partially supported and two hypotheses were not supported. Self-control has the most consistent and the most significant impact on delinquency. The impact on self-control has been soundly documented by research; therefore, the findings in this study relating to self-control are as expected. The findings are consistent with the research that already exists on self-control. The race related findings add to the limited research on self-control that analyzes minorities. An unexpected finding is the relationship between self-control and vandalism for African Americans, which was not significant using OLS regression. However, the expected significant inverse relationship remains consistent when logistic regression is used. Overall, self-control maintains its reputation for being the undisputed best predictor of delinquency.

Social bonding is believed to be pivotal in the process that leads to the development of self-control. Four measures were used for social bonding – parental supervision, family attachment, school attachment, and involvement in conventional pursuits. Involvement in conventional pursuits did not prove to be a good measure of social bonding in the expected direction. In fact, it had the opposite effect, contributing to an increase in delinquency instead of the expected decrease. Theoretically, this may be explained by an increase in opportunity resulting from involvement in activities away from home. Depending on whether logistic regression or OLS regression is used, family attachment and school attachment are significant predictors of delinquency. Parental supervision did not produce the expected significance. Perhaps the strength of parental supervision was diminished by other variables, especially family attachment. Native Americans are most affected by the influence of parental supervision when logistic regression is used. However, when OLS regression is used that significance is lost. Property, vandalism and substance/drug use were decreased by parental supervision for Native Americans. Self-esteem did not stand the test of significance as a predictor of delinquency, except as it relates to an increase in delinquency, specifically for African Americans. However, it has a positive relationship with self-control. Additional research will be required before any definitive conclusions can be drawn.

Interesting findings resulted when self-esteem was examined as a dependent variable. One of these findings is depicted in Figure 1 where a positive relationship exists between delinquency and self-esteem with increased delinquency causing an increase in self-esteem. This was observed in the relationship between delinquency and self-esteem for African Americans. Each type of delinquency was positively related to self-esteem. In addition, self-control was positively related to self-esteem across each type of delinquency for African Americans.

Table 11.1.   Support for Hypotheses

Hypothesis		Supported	Logistic	OLS
H1	Social bonding is negatively related to delinquency.	Partially	X	X
H2	Social bonding is positively related to self-control.	Partially		X
H3	Social bonding is positively related to self-esteem.	Yes		X
H4	The effect of social bonding on delinquency is mediated by self-esteem.	No	X	
H5	Self-control is negatively related to delinquency.	Yes	X	X
H6	The impact of social bonding on delinquency is mediated by self-control.	Partially	X	
H7	Self-control is positively related to self-esteem.	Yes		X
H8	Net of other predictors, self-esteem has a negative impact on delinquency.	No		
H9	The relative impacts of social bonding, self-control, and self-esteem on delinquency will vary by race.	Yes	X	X
H10	The relative impacts of social bonding, self-control, and delinquency on self-esteem will vary by race.	Yes		X
H11	Net of other predictors, delinquency has a positive impact on self-esteem.	Partially		X

Most Theoretically Important Findings

The significance of social bonding theory is confirmed in this research. Hirschi (1969) identified attachment as the cornerstone for social bonding, and the present research found attachment to family to be the most significant social bonding indicator for decreasing the prevalence of delinquency, followed by school attachment and parental supervision. A positive relationship between social bonding and self-control was hypothesized. Social bonding to parents or guardians at an early age is believed to increase the likelihood of developing self-control later in life. Social bonding in the present study is positively related to self-control. This represents an extension of the research by Gottfredson and Hirschi (1990), who did not link the two theories. The findings here indicate a possible link between social bonding and self-control as proposed by Akers (2000). Akers believed the two theories represented parts of a comprehensive perspective that would more adequately explain the development of delinquency.

Consistent with prior research (Kaplan, 1982; Wells and Rankin, 1983; Wells, 1989; Rosenberg et al., 1989), the findings on self-esteem are mixed. Overall, support was found for the positive relationship between self-esteem and delinquency, but no significance was found for the inverse relationship. Some interesting and surprising findings were generated when self-esteem was used as the dependent variable. The impact of parental supervision was maximized because it was the only predictor that has a consistent positive impact on self-esteem for each race, across each type of delinquency. The significance remained consistent when controlling for other predictors and control variables, as well as for delinquency. Parental supervision has a positive effect on self-esteem, controlling for each type of delinquency separately and together. These findings lend support for the significant role of parental supervision in relation to delinquency advocated by Gottfredson and Hirschi (1990).

African Americans' self-esteem remains an important issue and warrants additional study. Some argue that African Americans and Whites do not differ in self-esteem (Cross, 1991; Porter and Washington, 1989), while others say they do differ, and that racism has produced identity problems, anger and rage among African Americans, as well as psychopathology (Cose, 1993; Thomas and Hughes, 1998). This research did find significant racial variation in self-esteem as a predictor of delinquency when OLS regression was used and when self-esteem was the dependent variable. Whites in this research have higher self-esteem than either African Americans or Native Americans. The findings on self-esteem represent an extension of the existing research on self-esteem, specifically as it relates to African Americans. A positive relationship was observed between self-esteem and delinquency for African Americans. This is the positive relationship described in Figure 1, which reflects the ongoing debate about whether greater self-esteem decreases delinquency, or conversely, delinquency enhances self-esteem. The findings in this research indicate that African American is the only racial group for which delinquency has a positive effect on self-esteem.

In addition, unlike the results for other groups, average grade and school attachment have no significant impact on self-esteem for African Americans. In fact, logistic regression analysis revealed a positive relationship between average grade and interpersonal delinquency for African Americans. However, a significant inverse relationship was observed between average grade and vandalism for African Americans. An increase in average grades translates into a 40 percent decrease in the likelihood of vandalism for African Americans. This implies the significance that success in school has for African Americans in relation to this form of delinquency. Kaplan has studied the relationship between school success and delinquency for African Americans. Kaplan's general theory model (1986), in which he links self-rejection and general deviance, may help explain the counter-intuitive relationship between school success and delinquency. School failure is considered to be a specific type of deviant behavior. Kaplan explains the relationship between self-rejection and school failure as one that depends on an association of self-derogation with perceptions of rejection and failure in school (Kaplan, 1982, 1986). This association decreases the motivation to conform and increases the motivation to deviate from conventional norms.

Kaplan and Mitchell (1994) expanded the model to reflect what happens when students link their negative "self-feelings" and the school environment. The students develop attitudes and defenses that protect or enhance their self-esteem by adopting self-handicapping strategies, such as nonparticipation in school. This type of behavior ensures their failure, and they can attribute the failure to their own lack of effort, over which they feel they have full power and control, rather than to a lack of ability, over which they feel they have no control. The outcome of both of these scenarios is a child who does not like school. Not liking school is a predictor of delinquency (Gottfredson and Hirschi, 1990; Glueck and Glueck, 1950). School performance is also a predictor of involvement in delinquent activities, and those who do well in school are less likely to get in trouble with the law because they perceive a successful future and are more amenable to school sanctions (Gottfredson and Hirschi, 1990).

The positive relationship between average grade and interpersonal delinquency for African Americans may be explained by cultural differences. Making good grades may antagonize peers and create strain in relationships that adolescents cannot deal with effectively (Brezina, 2000). However, a negative relationship is observed between school attachment and delinquency, which indicates that school climates may play an important role in achievement for African Americans. Those schools that have high expectations and advocate high achievement for all students may significantly impact the relationship between average grade and delinquency. This is an area that warrants additional study because school attachment is the social bonding measure with the strongest inverse effect on delinquency for African Americans. Research has identified school attachment as a primary predictor of delinquency (Glueck and Glueck, 1950; Nye, 1958; Kaplan, 1978, 1982, 1986, 1994; Gottfredson and Hirschi, 1990).

Similar findings were observed for Native Americans, in which there was no significant association between school attachment and self-esteem. The cultural discontinuity thesis is another possible explanation for what minorities experience in this country. According to this thesis, the difference in cultural beliefs of some minorities from those of the White majority makes assimilation within American society difficult, especially within the public school system (Wood and Clay, 1996). They reject the dominant culture's norms and values instead of embracing them. Consequently, Native Americans and African Americans may eventually view themselves as members of a "devalued" social group. This model includes personal self-evaluation, perceived devaluation by others based on social group membership, and attitudes and behaviors resulting from socialization as a member of a devalued social group (Katz et al., 2002). Collective identities may impact the self-esteem and emotional well being of ethnic minorities if they perceive that their group is devalued by the dominant culture

(Cross, 1991; Luhtanen and Crocker, 1992; Katz et al., 2002). Cross (1991) contends that some African Americans learn to value Whites and to devalue their own group, which is also a form of self-derogation that relates back to Kaplan's delinquency hypothesis. In addition, similar self-derogation may take place in reference to African Americans' life chances, specifically as they relate to skin color (Hughes and Hertel, 1990; Hughes and Thomas, 1998; Hill, 2000).

Gender and Self-Esteem

This research is exploratory. Discovering unexpected relationships is one of the outcomes of exploratory research. This section is added to highlight the unexpected finding between gender and self-esteem for African Americans. In addition, information is explored to explain why this relationship may exist. Findings in this research indicate stronger self-esteem among African American females than African American males. Most research on gender and self-esteem reports stronger self-esteem for males (Ellison, 1993; Hoelter, 1983). Native Americans and Whites followed this predicted pattern but not African Americans. Black females register higher self-esteem than do males even when controlling for other factors. The traditional role of African American females may account for some of this discrepancy. Traditionally, African American women had to be more autonomous and independent than other women, which may explain the increase in their level of self-esteem. Though not examined in this study, personal mastery may also play a role in the difference in self-esteem development for African American women. Personal mastery refers to the perceived ability of the individual to attain goals and overcome obstacles (Ellison, 1993:1044). Ellison's findings indicate a positive relationship between personal mastery and self-esteem, which may explain why African American females would have higher self-esteem than African American males. African Americans do not experience the same level of personal mastery as Whites (Hughes and Thomas, 1998), but African American females are more successful in school and have often been able to obtain jobs when African American males could not.

High unemployment and incarceration rates among African American males impinge upon their ability to realize personal mastery. Limited job opportunities and living conditions of many young African American males place them at risk for becoming involved in crime.

According to research there is an association between joblessness and violent and other crimes in neighborhoods with joblessness (Sampson and Lauritsen, 1997; Messner et al., 2001; Morenoff et al., 2001). Mass imprisonment has changed the life course of African American males (Pettit and Western, 2004). An African American male high school dropout born between 1965 and 1969 had nearly a 60 percent chance of serving time in prison by the end of 1990s. The risk for serving time in prison is six to eight times higher for young African American men compared to young Whites (Pettit and Western, 2004). This same research found that an increase risk of imprisonment also exists for black males who completed only twelve years of education.

The present study supports prior research by Gottfredson and Hirschi (1990) on self-control. The inverse relationship between self-control and delinquency was found to be consistent across each type of delinquency. The race related findings extend the available research on self-control, specifically by revealing that African Americans are the only group for which self-control has a positive effect on self-esteem.

Limitations of the Study

The limitations of this study include data that are not from a representative sample. It is not a random sample; therefore, generalizing the findings of this study to the population at large should be undertaken with caution. This study is exploratory in nature; consequently, it may not offer all of the expected explanations for why members of the included racial groups participate in delinquency. In addition, the use of self-reported data contributes to questions about validity as well as reliability. The primary concerns are whether respondents alter their true responses for reasons that include social desirability, to potential researcher bias in administering the survey.

Another limitation of the study is the sample size. Although Native Americans are overrepresented, the number of African Americans included in the sample is not representative of the population. Therefore, the regression coefficients may not reflect the full extent of significance in the tested hypotheses for African Americans. Males are also under represented in this sample (43.3%), and females are overrepresented (56.6%).

Some of the scales that have not been used in prior research may also present questionable results, especially the scale used to measure involvement in conventional pursuits, since the Cronbach's alpha score was relatively low. It is highly probable that other combinations of behaviors would produce difference results. In addition, the similarity between the concepts of family attachment and parental supervision may affect the findings for both concepts.

The issue of tautology continues to surface, even though Gottfredson and Hirschi devoted considerable effort into explaining why it does not apply to self-control. Therefore, it will probably emerge as a limitation in this study. Grasmick and associates (1993) quieted the debate somewhat with their measures designed for more direct testing of the different dimensions of self-control. Still, there are questions asked regarding using an attitudinal scale that asks respondents about their behavior to explain behavior (Akers, 2000). This research may also present mediating effects of self-control, specifically when examining parental supervision and family attachment.

Finally, the use of the chosen theoretical frameworks and the exploratory nature of this research decrease confidence in the final results specifically, since controls were not used for competing theories of delinquency, such as differential association, strain, or social learning that specify known correlates.

Policy Implications

More research is necessary before any definitive policy implications can be strongly recommended. This study emphasizes the need for a better understanding of the significance of prevention and early intervention during the early years of childhood; however, the above limitations restrict the policy implications of this study. Therefore, the implications discussed here are to be considered with circumspection. There are some implications for more emphasis on effective parenting and ways to improve social bonding. A social bonding model that has accomplished some desirable goals is the Social Development Model (S.D.M.) developed and implemented by J. David Hawkins and his associates in Seattle, Washington (Akers, 2000). The program, which has resulted in moderate success, is designed to train parents to effectively monitor their children, to teach normative expectations, and to provide appropriate and consistent discipline. The group receiving intervention scored higher on commitment and attachment to school, and was somewhat less likely than the control group to have engaged in alcohol use and other deviant behavior. The greatest difference was observed in self-reported violent delinquency (Akers, 2000). The project supports Gottfredson and Hirschi's theoretical suppositions in the form of applied research. The implications of the project are supported by this study. Public institutions including religious, educational and governmental, should consider ways to expose parishioners, students and parents who receive governmental assistance to the principles advocated in social bonding theory.

Policy implications of self-control are inherent in social bonding activities. Policies intending to impact self-control must be implemented early in the child's life, since self-control develops in the family through childhood socialization. Gottfredson and Hirschi (1990) describe the recommended socialization as prevention rather than treatment. The simplicity of the recommendations by Gottfredson and Hirschi removes the need for prolonged debates because most people believe in family and few will have any difficulty accepting the merit of increasing bonding of children to parents in order to improve the likelihood that children will develop self-control.

Future Research

Social bonding and self-control theories are not the only theoretical frameworks that are applicable to the study of delinquency. Additional research using other theories such as strain, differential association or social learning theory, and social class may produce different results.

A primary consideration for future researchers is to use data that are culturally diverse with adequate numbers in the minority groups that are used for comparison. In the times that we live in today it is more than an oversight to continue to do serious research without examining group comparisons. Future researchers should make a special effort to include Hispanics as well as Native Americans and African Americans.

Additional research is recommended on the relationship that was observed between self-control and self-esteem, specifically for African Americans. The findings in reference to African Americans and self-esteem call for additional research to examine the positive relationship that was observed. Many questions are generated about this relationship beginning with why a positive relationship exists to what can be done about it. If self-control increases self-esteem and self-esteem increases delinquency for African-Americans, how will theory address this relationship?

Extended research on the counter-intuitive findings is recommended, specifically on why the involvement in conventional pursuits increases property delinquency and vandalism except for Native Americans, and why African Americans who make good grades are more likely to participate in interpersonal delinquency.

This research only scratched the surface of theory integration; however, it is believed that enough significance was observed to warrant future research on the integration of social bonding and self-control theories.

Self-Control Scale

Responses were recoded: 1= strongly disagree, 2 = disagree somewhat, 3 = agree somewhat, and 4 = strongly agree

1. I don't devote much thought and effort to preparing for the future.
2. I often do whatever brings me pleasure here and now even at the cost of some distant goal.
3. I'm more concerned with what happens to me in the short run than in the long run.
4. I much prefer doing things that pay off right away rather than in the future.
5. I frequently try to avoid projects that I know will be difficult.
6. When things get complicated, I tend to quit or withdraw.
7. The things in life that are easiest to do bring me the most pleasure.
8. I dislike really hard tasks that stretch my abilities to the limit.
9. I like to test myself every now and then by doing something a little risky.
10. Sometimes I will take a risk just for the fun of it.
11. I sometimes find it exciting to do things for which I might get in trouble.
12. Excitement and adventure are more important to me than peace and security.
13. If I had a choice, I would almost always rather do something physical rather than something mental.
14. I almost always feel better when I am on the move rather than sitting and thinking.
15. I like to get out and do things more than I like to read or think about things.
16. I seem to have more energy and a greater need for activity than most other people my age.

17. I try to look out for myself first, even if it means making things difficult for other people.
18. I'm not very sympathetic to other people when they are having problems.
19. If things upset other people, it's their problem not mine.
20. I will try to get the things I want even when I know it's causing problems for other people.
21. I lose my temper pretty easily.
22. Often when I'm angry at people I feel more like hurting them than talking to them about why I'm angry.
23. When I am really angry other people better stay away from me.
24. When I have a serious disagreement with someone, it's usually hard for me to talk calmly about it without getting upset.

Factor Analysis

Table 1. Factor Analysis (Delinquency)

Factor Loading	Alpha		Alpha if Deleted
Interpersonal			
Hit	.793		.7386
Fight	.846		.6796
Group	.650	.7735	.7629
Hurt	.735		.7342
Gun	.798		.7328
Property			
Taken	.772		.4699
Stolen	.707		.5735
Shoplift	.714	.6179	.5095
Joyride	.243		.6810
Car	.769		.5373
Vandalism			
Damage	.754		.7594
House	.868		.7385
Fire	.852	.8043	.7470
School	.544		.8342
Work	.814		.7545
Substance/Drug Use			
Smoke	.555		.8560
Drink	.882		.6203
Drunk	.902	.7379	.6349
Toke	.818		.6652
Drugs	.714		.7261

Table 2. **Factor Analysis (Predictors)**

Factor Loading	Alpha	Alpha if Deleted
Self-Esteem		
Esteem1	.742	.6747
Esteem2	.635	.7117
Esteem3	.640	.6941
Esteem4	.593	.7367	.7194
Esteem5	.700	.6815
Esteem6	.607	.7158
Esteem7	.528	.7411
Parental Supervision		
Monitor	.727	.6021
Recognize	.816	.6408	.4545
Punished	.749	.5721
Family Attachment		
CPI31	.609	.6874
CPI37	.639	.6785
CPI55	.623	.6847
CPI79	.582	.7162	.6949
CPI80	.708	.6573
CPI69	.695	.6618
School Attachment		
Enjoy	.739	.7600
Dowell	.511	.8007
Like School	.783	.7966	.7463
School Work	.730	.7558
Courses	.762	.7485
Learn	.689	.7725
Involvement		
Affairs	.373	.5535
Music	.531	.5204
Sports	.420	.5452
Art	.443	.5578	.5375
Write	.575	.5165
Yard	.542	.5046
Read	.630	.4774
Shop	.481	.5290

OLS Regression with Self-Esteem as the Dependent Variable

Table 1. OLS Regression, Full Model, Predictors, Interpersonal and Self-Esteem as Dependent Variable

	B	S.E.	β	t	Sig.†
(Constant)	8.831	1.580		5.591	.000
Interpersonal	.043*	.015	.069	2.797	.003
Parental Super.	.337*	.051	.163	6.651	.000
School Attach.	.088*	.025	.094	3.501	.000
Family Attach.	.359*	.051	.191	6.997	.000
Involvement	.006*	.003	.051	2.060	.020
Self-Control	.013	.008	.045	1.551	.061
Average Grade	.636*	.109	.153	5.811	.000
Age	.310*	.083	.092	3.754	.000
Female[a]	-.438*	.180	-.060	-2.429	.008
df	9				
R^2	.18				
Adjusted R^2	.18				
Number	1441				

*$p<.05$, †one-tailed significance level, [a] reference category = male

Table 2. OLS Regression, Full Model, Predictors, Property
and Self-Esteem as Dependent Variable

	B	S.E.	β	t	Sig.†
(Constant)	8.837	1.606		5.502	.000
Property	.021*	.010	.054	2.083	.019
Parental Super.	.335*	.051	.162	6.510	.000
School Attach.	.093*	.025	.100	3.676	.000
Family Attach.	.359*	.052	.191	6.875	.000
Involvement	.005*	.003	.044	1.746	.041
Self-Control	.014	.009	.046	1.582	.057
Average Grade	.631*	.111	.151	5.658	.000
Age	.306*	.084	.091	3.652	.000
Female[a]	-.398*	.186	-.054	-2.143	.016
df	9				
R²	.18				
Adjusted R²	.17				
Number	1404				

*p<.05, †one-tailed significance level, [a] reference category = male

Table 3. OLS Regression, Full Model, Predictors, Vandalism
and Self-Esteem as Dependent Variable

	B	S.E.	β	t	Sig.†
(Constant)	9.389	1.607		5.843	.000
Vandalism	.013*	.010	.034	1.355	.000
Parental Super.	.322*	.051	.155	6.258	.000
School Attach.	.090*	.025	.097	3.568	.000
Family Attach.	.365*	.052	.193	7.020	.000
Involvement	.005*	.003	.042	1.683	.047
Self-Control	.012	.009	.041	1.390	.083
Average Grade	.616*	.112	.146	5.522	.000
Age	.295*	.084	.086	3.500	.000
Female[a]	-.414*	.183	-.056	-2.261	.024
df	9				
R²	.17				
Adjusted R²	.17				
Number	1434				

*p<.05, †one-tailed significance level, [a] reference category = male

Table 4. OLS Regression, Full Model, Predictors, Substance/ Drugs and Self-Esteem as Dependent Variable

	B	S.E.	β	t	Sig.†
(Constant)	9.046	1.584		5.710	.000
Substance/Drugs	.004	.004	.025	.943	.173
Parental Super.	.333*	.051	.161	6.574	.000
School Attach.	.094*	.025	.102	3.732	.000
Family Attach.	.360*	.052	.190	6.970	.000
Involvement	.005	.003	.039	1.585	.057
Self-Control	.012	.008	.041	1.436	.076
Average Grade	.588*	.111	.140	5.316	.000
Age	.307*	.084	.090	3.670	.000
Female[a]	-.420*	.182	-.057	-2.315	.011
df	9				
R^2	.17				
Adjusted R^2	.17				
Number	1462				

*$p<.05$, †one-tailed significance level, [a] reference category = male

Table 5. OLS Regression, Full Model, Predictors, All Delinquency Measures and Self-Esteem as Dependent Variable

	B	S.E.	β	t	Sig.†
(Constant)	7.893	1.651		4.780	.000
Interpersonal	.053*	.022	.066	2.416	.008
Property	.017	.012	.042	1.418	.078
Vandalism	-.013	.017	-.023	-.745	.229
Substance/Drugs	.001	.005	.004	.140	.446
Parental Super.	.359*	.053	.172	6.783	.000
School Attach.	.096*	.026	.102	3.669	.000
Family Attach.	.372*	.053	.197	7.004	.000
Involvement	.005*	.003	.045	1.778	.038
Self-Control	.015*	.009	.052	1.719	.043
Average Grade	.641*	.114	.152	5.633	.000
Age	.327*	.085	.096	3.823	.000
Female[a]	-.379*	.189	-.051	-2.011	.022
df	9				
R^2	.17				
Adjusted R^2	.17				
Number	1462				

$p<.05$, †one-tailed significance level, [a] reference category = male

Table 6. OLS Regression, Native American, Predictors,
Interpersonal and Self-Esteem as Dependent Variable

	B	S.E.	β	t	Sig.†
(Constant)	8.013	3.133		2.557	.006
Interpersonal	.013	.042	.016	.302	.382
Parental Super.	.427*	.097	.234	4.389	.000
School Attach.	-.024	.053	-.025	-.454	.326
Family Attach.	.483*	.120	.245	4.044	.000
Involvement	-.001	.006	-.013	-.251	.401
Self-Control	-.005	.017	-.017	-.271	.394
Average Grade	.681*	.219	.170	3.106	.001
Age	.491*	.164	.159	2.986	.002
Female[a]	-.658*	.388	-.091	-1.697	.046
df	9				
R^2	.24				
Adjusted R^2	.21				
Number	307				

*p<.05, †one-tailed significance level, [a] reference category = male

Table 7. OLS Regression, Native American, Predictors,
Property and Self-Esteem as Dependent Variable

	B	S.E.	β	t	Sig.†
(Constant)	7.512	3.190		2.355	.010
Property	.016	.015	.059	1.061	.145
Parental Super.	.384*	.097	.215	3.973	.000
School Attach.	.017	.052	.019	.334	.370
Family Attach.	.482*	.122	.244	3.949	.000
Involvement	-.003	.006	-.031	-.586	.279
Self-Control	-.004	.017	-.014	-.218	.414
Average Grade	.691*	.223	.170	3.102	.001
Age	.494*	.167	.158	2.952	.002
Female[a]	-.567	.393	-.078	-1.442	.075
df	9				
R^2	.23				
Adjusted R^2	.20				
Number	305				

*p<.05, †one-tailed significance level, [a] reference category = male

Table 8. OLS Regression, Native American, Predictors,
Vandalism and Self-Esteem as Dependent Variable

	B	S.E.	β	t	Sig.†
(Constant)	8.013	3.133		2.557	.006
Vandalism	.009	.011	.043	.805	.211
Parental Super.	.394*	.098	.218	4.019	.000
School Attach.	-.006	.054	-.007	-.118	.453
Family Attach.	.438*	.120	.225	3.654	.000
Involvement	-.002	.006	-.015	-.278	.391
Self-Control	-.003	.017	-.013	-.201	.421
Average Grade	.738*	.224	.182	3.293	.001
Age	.459*	.167	.148	2.742	.003
Female[a]	-.642*	.387	-.089	-1.661	.049
df	9				
R^2	.22				
Adjusted R^2	.20				
Number	308				

*p<.05, †one-tailed significance level, [a] reference category = male

Table 9. OLS Regression, Native American, Predictors,
Substance/ Drugs and Self-Esteem as Dependent Variable

	B	S.E.	β	t	Sig.†
(Constant)	7.120	3.093		2.302	.011
Substance/Drugs	.012	.008	.082	1.434	.077
Parental Super.	.423*	.096	.237	4.390	.000
School Attach.	.019	.052	.020	.359	.360
Family Attach.	.461*	.120	.235	3.850	.000
Involvement	-.002	.006	-.021	-.403	.344
Self-Control	-.002	.017	-.008	-.121	.452
Average Grade	.620*	.219	.154	2.834	.003
Age	.496*	.164	.160	3.016	.002
Female[a]	-.600	.383	-.083	-1.568	.059
df	9				
R^2	.23				
Adjusted R^2	.21				
Number	312				

*p<.05, †one-tailed significance level, [a] reference category = male

Table 10. OLS Regression, Native American, Predictors, All Delinquency Measures and Self-Esteem as Dependent Variable

	B	S.E.	β	t	Sig.†
(Constant)	6.855	3.295		2.080	.019
Interpersonal	-.003	.054	-.003	-.060	.476
Property	.018	.017	.064	1.075	.142
Vandalism	-.017	.024	-.048	-.728	.234
Substance/Drugs	.010	.012	.057	.856	.196
Parental Super.	.414*	.102	.229	4.062	.000
School Attach.	.016	.056	.016	.283	.389
Family Attach.	.529*	.124	.266	4.270	.000
Involvement	-.002	.006	-.016	-.296	.384
Self-Control	-.002	.018	-.008	-.125	.451
Average Grade	.705*	.229	.173	3.085	.001
Age	.487*	.173	.156	2.820	.003
Female[a]	-.532	.405	-.073	-1.312	.095
df	12				
R^2	.26				
Adjusted R^2	.22				
Number	291				

*p<.05, †one-tailed significance level, [a] reference category = male

Table 11. OLS Regression, African American, Predictors, Interpersonal and Self-Esteem as Dependent Variable

	B	S.E.	β	t	Sig.†
(Constant)	8.650	5.204		1.662	.050
Interpersonal	.051*	.022	.176	2.297	.012
Parental Super.	.391*	.155	.205	2.522	.007
School Attach.	.019	.079	.019	.239	.406
Family Attach.	.326*	.188	.142	1.736	.043
Involvement	.013	.009	.115	1.506	.067
Self-Control	.044*	.026	.148	1.704	.045
Average Grade	.325	.387	.066	.839	.202
Age	.240	.268	.067	.897	.186
Female[a]	1.654*	.618	.200	2.677	.004
df	9				
R^2	.22				
Adjusted R^2	.17				
Number	158				

p<.05, †one-tailed significance level, [a] reference category = male

Table 12. OLS Regression, African American, Predictors, Property and Self-Esteem as Dependent Variable

	B		β	t	Sig.†
(Constant)	10.032	5.445		1.842	.034
Property	.071*	.043	.137	1.664	.049
Parental Super.	.303*	.159	.160	1.907	.029
School Attach.	.037	.083	.038	.441	.330
Family Attach.	.272	.199	.119	1.368	.087
Involvement	.009	.009	.081	1.002	.159
Self-Control	.045*	.027	.150	1.656	.050
Average Grade	.419	.401	.086	1.044	.149
Age	.172	.278	.048	.619	.269
Female[a]	1.930*	.656	.233	2.94	.002
df	9				
R²	.18				
Adjusted R²	.13				
Number	151				

*p<.05, †one-tailed significance level, [a] reference category = male

Table 13. OLS Regression, African American, Predictors, Vandalism and Self-Esteem as Dependent Variable

	B	S.E.	β	t	Sig.†
(Constant)	9.614	5.304		1.813	.036
Vandalism	.111*	.053	.164	2.087	.020
Parental Super.	.379*	.159	.197	2.386	.009
School Attach.	.029	.081	.029	.360	.360
Family Attach.	.278	.190	.121	1.468	.072
Involvement	.015*	.009	.128	1.663	.049
Self-Control	.051*	.026	.170	1.950	.027
Average Grade	.302	.384	.062	.788	.216
Age	.155	.273	.043	.569	.285
Female[a]	1.764*	.618	.215	2.852	.003
df	9				
R²	.20				
Adjusted R²	.15				
Number	158				

*p<.05, †one-tailed significance level, [a] reference category = male

Table 14. OLS Regression, African American, Predictors, Substance/ Drugs , Self-Esteem as Dependent Variable

	B	S.E.	β	t	Sig.†
(Constant)	12.307	4.956		2.483	.007
Substance/Drugs	.055*	.021	.212	2.675	.004
Parental Super.	.288*	.150	.152	1.922	.028
School Attach.	.007	076	.007	.087	.466
Family Attach.	.305*	.180	.136	1.693	.046
Involvement	.014*	.009	.124	1.656	.050
Self-Control	.048*	.025	.167	1.943	.027
Average Grade	.340	.374	.070	.908	.183
Age	.072	.263	.020	.275	.392
Female[a]	1.912*	.600	.238	3.185	.001
df	9				
R²	.21				
Adjusted R²	.16				
Number	164				

*p<.05, †one-tailed significance level, [a] reference category = male

Table 15. OLS Regression, African American, Predictors, All Measures and Self-Esteem as Dependent Variable

	B	S.E.	β	t	Sig.†
(Constant)	9.005	5.613		1.604	.056
Interpersonal	.077	.067	.189	1.145	.127
Property	-.041	.054	-.075	-.757	.225
Vandalism	.003	.121	.004	.025	.490
Substance/Drugs	.071*	.032	.188	2.204	.015
Parental Super.	.372*	.163	.194	2.290	.012
School Attach.	.050	.084	.051	.603	.274
Family Attach.	.293	.201	.127	1.458	.074
Involvement	.014	.010	.122	1.484	.070
Self-Control	.051*	.028	.171	1.858	.033
Average Grade	.256	.411	.052	.624	.267
Age	.155	.287	.043	.539	.296
Female[a]	1.971*	.678	.232	2.909	.002
df	12				
R²	.25				
Adjusted R²	.18				
Number	143				

*p<.05, †one-tailed significance level, [a] reference category = male

Table 16. OLS Regression, White, Predictors, Interpersonal and Self-Esteem as Dependent Variable

	B	S.E.	β	t	Sig.†
(Constant)	10.022	1.944		5.155	.000
Interpersonal	.003	.031	.003	.092	.464
Parental Super.	.282*	.065	.128	4.336	.000
School Attach.	.133*	.031	.146	4.315	.000
Family Attach.	.310*	.059	.172	5.238	.000
Involvement	.007*	.004	.060	2.011	.023
Self-Control	.009	.011	.031	.856	.196
Average Grade	.659*	.135	.159	4.879	.000
Age	.250*	.102	.073	2.455	.007
Female[a]	-.752*	.217	-.105	-3.462	.001
df	9				
R^2	.19				
Adjusted R^2	.18				
Number	974				

*$p<.05$, †one-tailed significance level, [a] reference category = male

Table 17. OLS Regression, White, Predictors, Property and Self-Esteem as Dependent Variable

	B	S.E.	β	t	Sig.†
(Constant)	9.400	1.977		4.755	.000
Property	.015	.015	.033	1.056	.146
Parental Super.	.316*	.067	.142	4.719	.000
School Attach.	.131*	.031	.143	4.208m	.000
Family Attach.	.316*	.060	.176	5.264	.000
Involvement	.007*	.004	.060	1.994	.023
Self-Control	.012	.011	.040	1.114	.133
Average Grade	.640*	.136	.154	4.695	.000
Age	.256*	.103	.075	2.494	.007
Female[a]	-.705*	.221	-.098	-3.185	.001
df	9				
R^2	.19				
Adjusted R^2	.19				
Number	946				

*$p<.05$, †one-tailed significance level, [a] reference category = male

Table 18.   OLS Regression, White, Predictors, Vandalism and
Self-Esteem as Dependent Variable

	B	S.E.	β	t	Sig.†
(Constant)	9.936	1.983		5.012	.000
Vandalism	.002	.021	.003	.108	.457
Parental Super.	.293*	.067	.130	4.392	.000
School Attach.	.133*	.031	.145	4.282	.000
Family Attach.	.334*	.060	.185	5.545	.000
Involvement	.005	.004	.045	1.500	.067
Self-Control	.010	.011	.033	.909	.182
Average Grade	.615*	.138	.146	4.472	.000
Age	.252*	.104	.072	2.425	.015
Female[a]	-.702*	.219	-.097	-3.201	.001
df	9				
R²	.19				
Adjusted R²	.18				
Number	966				

*p<.05, †one-tailed significance level, [a] reference category = male

Table 19.   OLS Regression, White, Predictors, Substance/
Drugs and Self-Esteem as Dependent Variable

	B	S.E.	β	t	Sig.†
(Constant)	9.818	1.965		4.996	.000
Substance/Drugs	-.001	.005	-.006	-.189	.425
Parental Super.	.301*	.066	.134	4.557	.000
School Attach.	.136*	.031	.147	4.340	.000
Family Attach.	.314*	.060	.172	5.227	.000
Involvement	.005	.004	.041	1.366	.086
Self-Control	.012	.011	.040	1.122	.131
Average Grade	.619*	.137	.147	4.522	.000
Age	.247*	.103	.071	2.389	.009
Female[a]	-.717*	.217	-.099	-3.305	.001
df	9				
R²	.19				
Adjusted R²	.18				
Number	984				

*p<.05, †one-tailed significance level, [a] reference category = male

Table 20. OLS Regression, White, Predictors, All
Delinquency Measures and Self-Esteem as Dependent Variable

	B	S.E.	β	t	Sig.†
(Constant)	9.021	2.031		4.441	.000
Interpersonal	.020	.040	.018	.497	.310
Property	.015	.018	.032	.820	.206
Vandalism	-.010	.028	-.014	-.348	.364
Substance/Drugs	-.001	.006	-.003	-093	.463
Parental Super.	.320*	.069	.141	4.669	.000
School Attach.	.131*	.032	.142	4.083	.000
Family Attach.	.323*	.061	.179	5.254	.000
Involvement	.007*	.004	.055	1.777	.038
Self-Control	.011	.011	.038	1.015	.156
Average Grade	.660*	.141	.157	4.690	.000
Age	.275*	.105	.080	2.620	.005
Female[a]	-.720*	.226	-.100	-3.181	.001
df	12				
R²	.19				
Adjusted R²	.18				
Number	926				

*p<.05, †one-tailed significance level, [a] reference category = male

Frequencies

RACE

		Frequency	Percent	Valid Percent	Cumulative Percent
Valid	Indian	382	22.2	22.2	22.2
	Black	220	12.8	12.8	34.9
	White	1122	65.1	65.1	100.0
	Total	1724	100.0	100.0	

WHITES

		Frequency	Percent	Valid Percent	Cumulative Percent
Valid	.00	602	34.9	34.9	34.9
	1.00	1122	65.1	65.1	100.0
	Total	1724	100.0	100.0	

INDIANS

		Frequency	Percent	Valid Percent	Cumulative Percent
Valid	.00	1342	77.8	77.8	77.8
	1.00	382	22.2	22.2	100.0
	Total	1724	100.0	100.0	

BLACKS

		Frequency	Percent	Valid Percent	Cumulative Percent
Valid	.00	1504	87.2	87.2	87.2
	1.00	220	12.8	12.8	100.0
	Total	1724	100.0	100.0	

GENDER

		Frequency	Percent	Valid Percent	Cumulative Percent
Valid	male	747	43.3	43.4	43.4
	female	975	56.6	56.6	100.0
	Total	1722	99.9	100.0	
Missing	9	2	.1		
Total		1724	100.0		

MALES

		Frequency	Percent	Valid Percent	Cumulative Percent
Valid	.00	975	56.6	56.6	56.6
	1.00	747	43.3	43.4	100.0
	Total	1722	99.9	100.0	
Missing	System	2	.1		
Total		1724	100.0		

FEMALES

		Frequency	Percent	Valid Percent	Cumulative Percent
Valid	**.00**	747	43.3	43.4	43.4
	1.00	975	56.6	56.6	100.0
	Total	1722	99.9	100.0	
Missing	**System**	2	.1		
Total		1724	100.0		

Family Attachment

		Frequency	Percent	Valid Percent	Cumulative Percent
Valid	**.00**	193	11.2	11.9	11.9
	1.00	262	15.2	16.1	27.9
	2.00	253	14.7	15.5	43.5
	3.00	265	15.4	16.3	59.8
	4.00	251	14.6	15.4	75.2
	5.00	214	12.4	13.1	88.3
	6.00	190	11.0	11.7	100.0
	Total	1628	94.4	100.0	
Missing	**System**	96	5.6		
Total		1724	100.0		

Parental Supervision

		Frequency	Percent	Valid Percent	Cumulative Percent
Valid	3.00	8	.5	.5	.5
	4.00	9	.5	.5	1.0
	5.00	13	.8	.8	1.8
	6.00	31	1.8	1.8	3.6
	7.00	63	3.7	3.7	7.3
	8.00	118	6.8	6.9	14.2
	9.00	249	14.4	14.6	28.7
	10.00	255	14.8	14.9	43.6
	11.00	353	20.5	20.6	64.3
	12.00	611	35.4	35.7	100.0
	Total	1710	99.2	100.0	
Missing	System	14	.8		
Total		1724	100.0		

Monitor

		Frequency	Percent	Valid Percent	Cumulative Percent
Valid	Strongly disagree	957	55.5	55.9	55.9
	Disagree somewhat	539	31.3	31.5	87.4
	Agree somewhat	144	8.4	8.4	95.9
	Strongly agree	71	4.1	4.1	100.0
	Total	1711	99.2	100.0	
Missing	System	13	.8		
Total		1724	100.0		

Recognize

		Frequency	Percent	Valid Percent	Cumulative Percent
Valid	Strongly disagree	1022	59.3	59.8	59.8
	Disagree somewhat	517	30.0	30.2	90.0
	Agree somewhat	132	7.7	7.7	97.7
	Strongly agree	39	2.3	2.3	100.0
	Total	1710	99.2	100.0	
Missing	System	14	.8		
Total		1724	100.0		

Discipline

		Frequency	Percent	Valid Percent	Cumulative Percent
Valid	Strongly disagree	1080	62.6	63.1	63.1
	Disagree somewhat	446	25.9	26.1	89.2
	Agree somewhat	121	7.0	7.1	96.3
	Strongly Agree	64	3.7	3.7	100.0
	Total	1711	99.2	100.0	
Missing	System	13	.8		
Total		1724	100.0		

School Attachment

	Frequency	Percent	Valid Percent	Cumulative Percent
6.00	3	.2	.2	.2
7.00	1	.1	.1	.2
8.00	3	.2	.2	.4
9.00	11	.6	.6	1.1
10.00	14	.8	.8	1.9
11.00	29	1.7	1.7	3.6
12.00	23	1.3	1.3	4.9
13.00	46	2.7	2.7	7.6

School Attachment cont.

	14.00	47	2.7	2.8	10.4
	15.00	86	5.0	5.0	15.4
	16.00	84	4.9	4.9	20.3
	17.00	116	6.7	6.8	27.1
	18.00	144	8.4	8.4	35.5
	19.00	173	10.0	10.1	45.7
	20.00	197	11.4	11.5	57.2
	21.00	189	11.0	11.1	68.3
	22.00	163	9.5	9.5	77.8
	23.00	127	7.4	7.4	85.2
	24.00	99	5.7	5.8	91.0
	25.00	64	3.7	3.7	94.8
	26.00	48	2.8	2.8	97.6
	27.00	29	1.7	1.7	99.3
	28.00	12	.7	.7	100.0
	Total	1708	99.1	100.0	
Missing	**System**	16	.9		
	Total	1724	100.0		

Conventional Pursuits

		Frequency	Percent	Valid Percent	Cumulative Percent
Valid	**.00**	21	1.2	1.3	1.3
	1.00	3	.2	.2	1.5
	2.00	11	.6	.7	2.1
	3.00	13	.8	.8	2.9
	4.00	14	.8	.9	3.8
	5.00	23	1.3	1.4	5.2
	6.00	14	.8	.9	6.0
	7.00	22	1.3	1.3	7.4
	8.00	14	.8	.9	8.2
	9.00	22	1.3	1.3	9.6
	10.00	18	1.0	1.1	10.7
	11.00	22	1.3	1.3	12.0
	12.00	24	1.4	1.5	13.5
	13.00	29	1.7	1.8	15.2
	14.00	16	.9	1.0	16.2
	15.00	37	2.1	2.3	18.4
	16.00	22	1.3	1.3	19.8
	17.00	31	1.8	1.9	21.7
	18.00	13	.8	.8	22.5
	19.00	17	1.0	1.0	23.5
	20.00	24	1.4	1.5	25.0
	21.00	19	1.1	1.2	26.1
	22.00	12	.7	.7	26.8

Conventional Pursuits cont.

23.00	22	1.3	1.3	28.2
24.00	17	1.0	1.0	29.2
25.00	30	1.7	1.8	31.0
26.00	20	1.2	1.2	32.3
27.00	19	1.1	1.2	33.4
28.00	20	1.2	1.2	34.6
29.00	25	1.5	1.5	36.2
30.00	26	1.5	1.6	37.7
31.00	19	1.1	1.2	38.9
32.00	20	1.2	1.2	40.1
33.00	26	1.5	1.6	41.7
34.00	11	.6	.7	42.4
35.00	22	1.3	1.3	43.7
36.00	17	1.0	1.0	44.7
37.00	30	1.7	1.8	46.6
38.00	21	1.2	1.3	47.8
39.00	23	1.3	1.4	49.2
40.00	18	1.0	1.1	50.3
41.00	23	1.3	1.4	51.7
42.00	20	1.2	1.2	53.0
43.00	21	1.2	1.3	54.2
44.00	24	1.4	1.5	55.7
45.00	15	.9	.9	56.6
46.00	31	1.8	1.9	58.5
47.00	16	.9	1.0	59.5

Conventional Pursuits cont.

48.00	26	1.5	1.6	61.0
49.00	9	.5	.5	61.6
50.00	20	1.2	1.2	62.8
51.00	11	.6	.7	63.5
52.00	13	.8	.8	64.3
53.00	14	.8	.9	65.1
54.00	15	.9	.9	66.0
55.00	15	.9	.9	67.0
56.00	14	.8	.9	67.8
57.00	15	.9	.9	68.7
58.00	18	1.0	1.1	69.8
59.00	11	.6	.7	70.5
60.00	21	1.2	1.3	71.8
61.00	18	1.0	1.1	72.9
62.00	8	.5	.5	73.3
63.00	21	1.2	1.3	74.6
64.00	14	.8	.9	75.5
65.00	10	.6	.6	76.1
66.00	12	.7	.7	76.8
67.00	8	.5	.5	77.3
68.00	12	.7	.7	78.0
69.00	15	.9	.9	78.9
70.00	10	.6	.6	79.5
71.00	5	.3	.3	79.9
72.00	9	.5	.5	80.4

Conventional Pursuits cont.

73.00	9	.5	.5	80.9
74.00	11	.6	.7	81.6
75.00	11	.6	.7	82.3
76.00	13	.8	.8	83.1
77.00	10	.6	.6	83.7
78.00	12	.7	.7	84.4
79.00	7	.4	.4	84.8
80.00	11	.6	.7	85.5
81.00	6	.3	.4	85.9
82.00	14	.8	.9	86.7
83.00	11	.6	.7	87.4
84.00	7	.4	.4	87.8
85.00	5	.3	.3	88.1
86.00	11	.6	.7	88.8
87.00	6	.3	.4	89.2
88.00	6	.3	.4	89.5
89.00	5	.3	.3	89.8
90.00	10	.6	.6	90.4
91.00	5	.3	.3	90.7
92.00	6	.3	.4	91.1
93.00	6	.3	.4	91.5
94.00	8	.5	.5	92.0
95.00	5	.3	.3	92.3
96.00	4	.2	.2	92.5
97.00	5	.3	.3	92.8

Conventional Pursuits cont.

98.00	5	.3	.3	93.1
99.00	10	.6	.6	93.7
100.00	5	.3	.3	94.0
101.00	6	.3	.4	94.4
102.00	4	.2	.2	94.6
103.00	6	.3	.4	95.0
104.00	10	.6	.6	95.6
105.00	4	.2	.2	95.9
106.00	2	.1	.1	96.0
107.00	3	.2	.2	96.2
108.00	1	.1	.1	96.2
109.00	3	.2	.2	96.4
110.00	3	.2	.2	96.6
111.00	6	.3	.4	97.0
112.00	2	.1	.1	97.1
113.00	2	.1	.1	97.2
114.00	1	.1	.1	97.3
115.00	4	.2	.2	97.5
116.00	4	.2	.2	97.7
117.00	2	.1	.1	97.9
118.00	2	.1	.1	98.0
121.00	3	.2	.2	98.2
122.00	1	.1	.1	98.2
123.00	1	.1	.1	98.3
124.00	3	.2	.2	98.5

Conventional Pursuits cont.

125.00	1	.1	.1	98.5
126.00	1	.1	.1	98.6
127.00	3	.2	.2	98.8
129.00	1	.1	.1	98.8
131.00	5	.3	.3	99.1
133.00	2	.1	.1	99.3
134.00	1	.1	.1	99.3
140.00	2	.1	.1	99.5
142.00	2	.1	.1	99.6
147.00	1	.1	.1	99.6
152.00	1	.1	.1	99.7
155.00	1	.1	.1	99.8
168.00	2	.1	.1	99.9
170.00	1	.1	.1	99.9
175.00	1	.1	.1	100.0
Total	1643	95.3	100.0	
Missing System	81	4.7		
Total	1724	100.0		

Self-Control

		Frequency	Percent	Valid Percent	Cumulative Percent
Valid	24.00	2	.1	.1	.1
	26.00	1	.1	.1	.2
	27.00	1	.1	.1	.2
	28.00	1	.1	.1	.3
	29.00	1	.1	.1	.4
	30.00	1	.1	.1	.4
	31.00	1	.1	.1	.5
	32.00	6	.3	.4	.9
	33.00	4	.2	.2	1.1
	34.00	2	.1	.1	1.2
	36.00	6	.3	.4	1.6
	37.00	1	.1	.1	1.7
	38.00	4	.2	.2	1.9
	39.00	10	.6	.6	2.5
	40.00	12	.7	.7	3.3
	41.00	10	.6	.6	3.9
	42.00	14	.8	.9	4.8
	43.00	13	.8	.8	5.6
	44.00	15	.9	.9	6.5
	45.00	16	.9	1.0	7.5
	46.00	16	.9	1.0	8.5
	47.00	11	.6	.7	9.2
	48.00	33	1.9	2.0	11.2

Self-Control cont.

49.00	28	1.6	1.7	12.9
50.00	29	1.7	1.8	14.7
51.00	34	2.0	2.1	16.8
52.00	46	2.7	2.8	19.7
53.00	39	2.3	2.4	22.1
54.00	39	2.3	2.4	24.5
55.00	42	2.4	2.6	27.1
56.00	39	2.3	2.4	29.5
57.00	60	3.5	3.7	33.2
58.00	52	3.0	3.2	36.4
59.00	58	3.4	3.6	40.0
60.00	67	3.9	4.1	44.2
61.00	53	3.1	3.3	47.5
62.00	38	2.2	2.4	49.8
63.00	45	2.6	2.8	52.6
64.00	59	3.4	3.7	56.3
65.00	41	2.4	2.5	58.8
66.00	47	2.7	2.9	61.7
67.00	55	3.2	3.4	65.1
68.00	47	2.7	2.9	68.0
69.00	36	2.1	2.2	70.2
70.00	42	2.4	2.6	72.8
71.00	36	2.1	2.2	75.1
72.00	44	2.6	2.7	77.8
73.00	40	2.3	2.5	80.3

Self-Control cont.

74.00	38	2.2	2.4	82.6
75.00	39	2.3	2.4	85.0
76.00	30	1.7	1.9	86.9
77.00	25	1.5	1.5	88.4
78.00	18	1.0	1.1	89.5
79.00	21	1.2	1.3	90.8
80.00	17	1.0	1.1	91.9
81.00	18	1.0	1.1	93.0
82.00	13	.8	.8	93.8
83.00	15	.9	.9	94.7
84.00	18	1.0	1.1	95.9
85.00	13	.8	.8	96.7
86.00	12	.7	.7	97.4
87.00	5	.3	.3	97.7
88.00	3	.2	.2	97.9
89.00	8	.5	.5	98.4
90.00	6	.3	.4	98.8
91.00	6	.3	.4	99.1
92.00	6	.3	.4	99.5
93.00	4	.2	.2	99.8
94.00	3	.2	.2	99.9
95.00	1	.1	.1	100.0
Total	1616	93.7	100.0	
Missing System	108	6.3		
Total	1724	100.0		

Self-Esteem

		Frequency	Percent	Valid Percent	Cumulative Percent
Valid	7.00	5	.3	.3	.3
	9.00	1	.1	.1	.4
	10.00	4	.2	.2	.6
	11.00	2	.1	.1	.7
	12.00	4	.2	.2	.9
	13.00	12	.7	.7	1.7
	14.00	9	.5	.5	2.2
	15.00	13	.8	.8	3.0
	16.00	27	1.6	1.6	4.5
	17.00	40	2.3	2.4	6.9
	18.00	60	3.5	3.5	10.4
	19.00	85	4.9	5.0	15.5
	20.00	133	7.7	7.9	23.3
	21.00	129	7.5	7.6	30.9
	22.00	156	9.0	9.2	40.1
	23.00	153	8.9	9.0	49.2
	24.00	201	11.7	11.9	61.0
	25.00	204	11.8	12.0	73.1
	26.00	188	10.9	11.1	84.2
	27.00	134	7.8	7.9	92.1
	28.00	134	7.8	7.9	100.0
	Total	1694	98.3	100.0	
Missing	System	30	1.7		

Interpersonal Delinquency

		Frequency	Percent	Valid Percent	Cumulative Percent
Valid	.00	1052	61.0	63.3	63.3
	1.00	222	12.9	13.4	76.7
	2.00	101	5.9	6.1	82.7
	3.00	76	4.4	4.6	87.3
	4.00	58	3.4	3.5	90.8
	5.00	32	1.9	1.9	92.7
	6.00	25	1.5	1.5	94.2
	7.00	17	1.0	1.0	95.2
	8.00	8	.5	.5	95.7
	9.00	7	.4	.4	96.1
	10.00	10	.6	.6	96.8
	11.00	8	.5	.5	97.2
	12.00	5	.3	.3	97.5
	13.00	4	.2	.2	97.8
	14.00	7	.4	.4	98.2
	15.00	6	.3	.4	98.6
	17.00	1	.1	.1	98.6
	18.00	4	.2	.2	98.9
	19.00	1	.1	.1	98.9
	21.00	2	.1	.1	99.0
	22.00	1	.1	.1	99.1
	24.00	1	.1	.1	99.2
	25.00	1	.1	.1	99.2

Interpersonal Delinquency cont.

26.00	2	.1	.1	99.3
27.00	1	.1	.1	99.4
28.00	1	.1	.1	99.5
29.00	1	.1	.1	99.5
31.00	1	.1	.1	99.6
32.00	1	.1	.1	99.6
33.00	1	.1	.1	99.7
37.00	1	.1	.1	99.8
43.00	1	.1	.1	99.8
48.00	1	.1	.1	99.9
115.00	1	.1	.1	99.9
118.00	1	.1	.1	100.0
Total	1662	96.4	100.0	
Missing System	62	3.6		
Total	1724	100.0		

Property Delinquency

	Frequency	Percent	Valid Percent	Cumulative Percent
Valid .00	870	50.5	54.0	54.0
1.00	210	12.2	13.0	67.0
2.00	110	6.4	6.8	73.8
3.00	70	4.1	4.3	78.2
4.00	57	3.3	3.5	81.7
5.00	54	3.1	3.3	85.0

Property Delinquency cont.

6.00	29	1.7	1.8	86.8
7.00	24	1.4	1.5	88.3
8.00	15	.9	.9	89.3
9.00	13	.8	.8	90.1
10.00	30	1.7	1.9	91.9
11.00	14	.8	.9	92.8
12.00	11	.6	.7	93.5
13.00	7	.4	.4	93.9
14.00	8	.5	.5	94.4
15.00	11	.6	.7	95.1
16.00	6	.3	.4	95.5
17.00	6	.3	.4	95.8
18.00	4	.2	.2	96.1
19.00	2	.1	.1	96.2
20.00	7	.4	.4	96.7
21.00	2	.1	.1	96.8
22.00	4	.2	.2	97.0
23.00	1	.1	.1	97.1
24.00	2	.1	.1	97.2
25.00	2	.1	.1	97.3
26.00	2	.1	.1	97.5
27.00	2	.1	.1	97.6
28.00	2	.1	.1	97.7
29.00	2	.1	.1	97.8
30.00	2	.1	.1	98.0

Property Delinquency cont.

31.00	2	.1	.1	98.1
32.00	3	.2	.2	98.3
33.00	2	.1	.1	98.4
35.00	2	.1	.1	98.5
36.00	1	.1	.1	98.6
37.00	1	.1	.1	98.6
39.00	2	.1	.1	98.8
43.00	1	.1	.1	98.8
44.00	1	.1	.1	98.9
45.00	1	.1	.1	98.9
47.00	1	.1	.1	99.0
49.00	1	.1	.1	99.1
50.00	1	.1	.1	99.1
52.00	1	.1	.1	99.2
54.00	1	.1	.1	99.3
57.00	1	.1	.1	99.3
60.00	1	.1	.1	99.4
61.00	1	.1	.1	99.4
63.00	1	.1	.1	99.5
69.00	1	.1	.1	99.6
74.00	2	.1	.1	99.7
77.00	1	.1	.1	99.8
85.00	1	.1	.1	99.8

Property Delinquency cont.

90.00	1	.1	.1	99.9
101.00	1	.1	.1	99.9
103.00	1	.1	.1	100.0
Total	1612	93.5	100.0	
Missing System	112	6.5		
Total	1724	100.0		

Vandalism

		Frequency	Percent	Valid Percent	Cumulative Percent
Valid	**.00**	1129	65.5	68.1	68.1
	1.00	185	10.7	11.2	79.3
	2.00	93	5.4	5.6	84.9
	3.00	48	2.8	2.9	87.8
	4.00	36	2.1	2.2	89.9
	5.00	36	2.1	2.2	92.1
	6.00	11	.6	.7	92.8
	7.00	26	1.5	1.6	94.3
	8.00	13	.8	.8	95.1
	9.00	6	.3	.4	95.5
	10.00	12	.7	.7	96.2
	11.00	5	.3	.3	96.5
	12.00	12	.7	.7	97.2
	13.00	3	.2	.2	97.4

Vandalism cont.

14.00	4	.2	.2	97.6
15.00	8	.5	.5	98.1
16.00	2	.1	.1	98.3
18.00	3	.2	.2	98.4
19.00	2	.1	.1	98.6
20.00	3	.2	.2	98.7
21.00	1	.1	.1	98.8
22.00	1	.1	.1	98.9
23.00	2	.1	.1	99.0
30.00	5	.3	.3	99.3
31.00	1	.1	.1	99.3
32.00	1	.1	.1	99.4
35.00	1	.1	.1	99.5
40.00	2	.1	.1	99.6
51.00	1	.1	.1	99.6
52.00	1	.1	.1	99.7
59.00	1	.1	.1	99.8
85.00	1	.1	.1	99.8
105.00	1	.1	.1	99.9
115.00	1	.1	.1	99.9
255.00	1	.1	.1	100.0
Total	1658	96.2	100.0	
Missing System	66	3.8		
Total	1724	100.0		

Substance/Drug Use

		Frequency	Percent	Valid Percent	Cumulative Percent
Valid	.00	699	40.5	42.2	42.2
	1.00	106	6.1	6.4	48.6
	2.00	84	4.9	5.1	53.7
	3.00	49	2.8	3.0	56.6
	4.00	57	3.3	3.4	60.1
	5.00	47	2.7	2.8	62.9
	6.00	28	1.6	1.7	64.6
	7.00	24	1.4	1.4	66.1
	8.00	30	1.7	1.8	67.9
	9.00	14	.8	.8	68.7
	10.00	21	1.2	1.3	70.0
	11.00	10	.6	.6	70.6
	12.00	21	1.2	1.3	71.9
	13.00	4	.2	.2	72.1
	14.00	15	.9	.9	73.0
	15.00	11	.6	.7	73.7
	16.00	9	.5	.5	74.2
	17.00	8	.5	.5	74.7
	18.00	12	.7	.7	75.4
	19.00	6	.3	.4	75.8
	20.00	17	1.0	1.0	76.8
	21.00	8	.5	.5	77.3

Substance/Drug Use cont.

22.00	7	.4	.4	77.7
23.00	3	.2	.2	77.9
24.00	8	.5	.5	78.4
25.00	9	.5	.5	78.9
26.00	5	.3	.3	79.2
27.00	1	.1	.1	79.3
28.00	43	2.5	2.6	81.9
29.00	18	1.0	1.1	83.0
30.00	18	1.0	1.1	84.1
31.00	15	.9	.9	85.0
32.00	12	.7	.7	85.7
33.00	13	.8	.8	86.5
34.00	15	.9	.9	87.4
35.00	10	.6	.6	88.0
36.00	17	1.0	1.0	89.0
37.00	5	.3	.3	89.3
38.00	9	.5	.5	89.9
39.00	5	.3	.3	90.2
40.00	4	.2	.2	90.4
41.00	4	.2	.2	90.6
42.00	5	.3	.3	90.9
43.00	2	.1	.1	91.1
44.00	14	.8	.8	91.9
45.00	7	.4	.4	92.3
46.00	8	.5	.5	92.8

Substance/Drug Use cont.

47.00	5	.3	.3	93.1
48.00	7	.4	.4	93.5
49.00	4	.2	.2	93.8
50.00	6	.3	.4	94.1
52.00	3	.2	.2	94.3
53.00	3	.2	.2	94.5
54.00	3	.2	.2	94.7
55.00	3	.2	.2	94.9
56.00	6	.3	.4	95.2
57.00	5	.3	.3	95.5
58.00	5	.3	.3	95.8
59.00	4	.2	.2	96.1
60.00	2	.1	.1	96.2
61.00	4	.2	.2	96.4
62.00	2	.1	.1	96.6
63.00	1	.1	.1	96.6
64.00	3	.2	.2	96.8
66.00	2	.1	.1	96.9
67.00	2	.1	.1	97.0
69.00	2	.1	.1	97.2
70.00	3	.2	.2	97.3
74.00	3	.2	.2	97.5
76.00	4	.2	.2	97.8
78.00	1	.1	.1	97.8
79.00	1	.1	.1	97.9

Substance/Drug Use cont.

80.00	2	.1	.1	98.0
83.00	2	.1	.1	98.1
84.00	2	.1	.1	98.2
87.00	1	.1	.1	98.3
88.00	1	.1	.1	98.4
89.00	1	.1	.1	98.4
91.00	2	.1	.1	98.6
92.00	1	.1	.1	98.6
94.00	1	.1	.1	98.7
98.00	1	.1	.1	98.7
103.00	1	.1	.1	98.8
104.00	1	.1	.1	98.9
106.00	2	.1	.1	99.0
109.00	2	.1	.1	99.1
111.00	1	.1	.1	99.2
112.00	3	.2	.2	99.3
113.00	1	.1	.1	99.4
116.00	1	.1	.1	99.5
117.00	2	.1	.1	99.6
127.00	1	.1	.1	99.6
132.00	2	.1	.1	99.8
140.00	4	.2	.2	100.0
Total	1656	96.1	100.0	
Missing System	68	3.9		
Total	1724	100.0		

AGE

		Frequency	Percent	Valid Percent	Cumulative Percent
Valid	15.00	72	4.2	4.2	4.2
	16.00	435	25.2	25.3	29.5
	17.00	598	34.7	34.8	64.3
	18.00	437	25.3	25.4	89.8
	19.00	156	9.0	9.1	98.8
	20.00	18	1.0	1.0	99.9
	21.00	2	.1	.1	100.0
	Total	1718	99.7	100.0	
Missing	System	6	.3		

Average Grade

		Frequency	Percent	Valid Percent	Cumulative Percent
Valid	1.00	181	10.5	10.5	10.5
	2.00	561	32.5	32.6	43.2
	3.00	720	41.8	41.9	85.0
	4.00	257	14.9	15.0	100.0
	Total	1719	99.7	100.0	
Missing	System	5	.3		
Total		1724	100.0		

Categorical recode of interpersonal delinquency

		Frequency	Percent	Valid Percent	Cumulative Percent
Valid	.00	1052	61.0	63.3	63.3
	1.00	610	35.4	36.7	100.0
	Total	1662	96.4	100.0	
Missing	System	62	3.6		
Total		1724	100.0		

Categorical recode of property delinquency

		Frequency	Percent	Valid Percent	Cumulative Percent
Valid	.00	870	50.5	54.0	54.0
	1.00	742	43.0	46.0	100.0
	Total	1612	93.5	100.0	
Missing	System	112	6.5		
Total		1724	100.0		

Categorical recode of substance/drugs delinquency

		Frequency	Percent	Valid Percent	Cumulative Percent
Valid	.00	699	40.5	42.2	42.2
	1.00	957	55.5	57.8	100.0
	Total	1656	96.1	100.0	
Missing	System	68	3.9		
Total		1724	100.0		

Categorical recode of vandalism

		Frequency	Percent	Valid Percent	Cumulative Percent
	.00	1129	65.5	68.1	68.1
Valid	1.00	529	30.7	31.9	100.0
	Total	1658	96.2	100.0	
Missing	System	66	3.8		
Total		1724	100.0		

Survey Instrument

These first few questions ask for some background information about yourself.

1. In what year were you born?
   19_ _ (write in the year)
2. What year in school are you? (Circle the number next to your answer)
   1. freshman
   2. sophomore
   3. junior
   4. senior
3. What is your sex?
   1. male
   2. female
4. How do you describe yourself?
   1. American Indian------------------------ What tribe or tribes _____
   2. Black or African American
   3. Mexican American
   4. Puerto Rican or other Latin American
   5. Asian or Asian-American
   6. White or Caucasian
   7. Other (specify) _____

Answer items 5 through 10 only if you identified yourself as an American Indian. If you are not an American Indian, go directly to question #11.

5. Are you enrolled as a federally recognized tribal member?
   1. yes
   2. no
   9. don't know
6. Thinking of your parents, was one or both of them American Indian?

        1.   just my mother
        2.   just my father
        3.   both of them
        9.   don't know

7.   Thinking of your four grandparents, how many of them were American Indians?
        1.   one of them
        2.   two of them
        3.   three of them
        4.   all four of them
        9.   don't know

8.   If someone asked you how much Indian blood you had, what would you tell them?
        1.   _____ Indian blood (use either a fraction or a percentage)
        9.   don't know

9.   The following section concerns your views on participation in American Indian culture and activities. Please circle your response to each of the statements below.
        1.   Strongly agree
        2.   Agree somewhat
        3.   Disagree somewhat
        4.   Strongly disagree

1 2 3 4   Attending pow-wows is an important part of American Indian lifestyle.

1 2 3 4   American Indian students should be knowledgeable about their heritage.

1 2 3 4   American Indians should learn to speak their native language/tongue.

1 2 3 4   More American Indians should attend Indian pow-wows.

1 2 3 4   It is important to belong to an Indian organization.

1 2 3 4   The American Indian medicine man is very important to American Indians.

1 2 3 4   American Indian studies are an important part of every Indian student's education.

1 2 3 4   American Indian political groups should help only American Indians.

1 2 3 4   American Indian parents should give their children Indian names.

1 2 3 4   What happens in my tribal community directly affects me.

    10. What was the percent of American Indian people in your: (Circle the number that best reflects your answer)

	None	1-25%	26-50%	51-75%	76-100%
a. Neighborhood 1	2	3	4	5	
b. Elementary School	1	2	3	4	5
c. Jr. high School	1	2	3	4	5
d. High School	1	2	3	4	5

All students should complete the rest of the survey.

    11. During most of your life did you live in a (circle your answer).

        1. Large city (more than 250,000)
        2. Suburb of a large city
        3. Medium city (50,000 to 250,000)
        4. Small city (10,000 to 50,000)
        5. Town (under 10,000)
        6. Rural area
        7. Reservation or Tribal lands.

Which of the following people live in the same household with you?

_____ Father (or male guardian)
_____ Mother (or female guardian)
_____ How many brothers?
_____ How many sisters?
_____ How many grandmother?
_____ How many grandfather?
_____ How many Aunts?
_____ How many Uncles?
_____ How many other relatives?

The next few questions ask about your parents. If you were raised mostly by foster-parents, step-parents, or others, answer for the one that was the most important in raising you.

What is the highest level of schooling your father completed?

        1.   8th grade or less
        2.   Some high school
        3.   Completed high school
        4.   Some college

5.   Completed college
6.   Graduate or professional school after college
9.   Don't Know

What is/was your father's most recent occupation?

1.   _____
9.   don't know

What does/did he actually do on that job? Please give a brief description.

_____

What is the highest level of schooling your mother completed?

1.   8th grade or less
2.   Some high school
3.   Completed high school
4.   Some college
5.   Completed college
6.   Graduate or professional school after college
9.   Don't know

What is/was your mother's most recent occupation?

1.   _____
9.   don't know

What does/did she actually do on that job? Please give a brief description.

_____

Did your mother have a paid job when you were growing up?

1.   No
2.   Yes, some of the time when I was growing up
3.   Yes, most of the time
4.   Yes, all or nearly all of the time

What is your religion? Are you Southern Baptist, Methodist, Catholic, or what? (Circle the number next to your religion)

00 no religion
01 Jewish
02 Catholic
03 Southern Baptist
04 Baptist (other than Southern Baptist)
05 Methodist
06 Church of Christ

07 Presbyterian
08 Christian Church
09 Episcopal
10 Church of God
11 Missouri Synod Lutheran
12 Lutheran (other than Missouri Synod)
13 Church of Nazarene
14 Assembly of God
15 Pentecostal
16 Jehovah's Witness
17 The Church of Jesus Christ of Latter Day Saints (Mormon)
18 Seventh-Day-Adventist
19 Christian Science
20 Native American Religion
21 other non-Protestant (SPECIFY: _____)
22 other Protestant (SPECIFY: _____)
About how many times per month do you attend religious services?
_____ times per month
How important is religion in your life?
    1. Not important
    2. A little important
    3. Pretty important
    4. Very important
For the next few items choose among the following four answers to tell how you feel about the statement. Circle the number that best expresses your position.
    1. strongly agree
    2. agree somewhat
    3. disagree somewhat
    4. strongly disagree
1 2 3 4   I take a positive attitude toward myself.
1 2 3 4   I am reliable.
1 2 3 4   I feel I do <u>not</u> have much to be proud of.
1 2 3 4   I am trustworthy.
1 2 3 4   On the whole, I am satisfied with myself.
1 2 3 4   When I do a job, I do it well.
1 2 3 4   I wish I could have more respect for myself.

How intelligent do you think you are compared with others your age?
1. Below average
2. Slightly below average
3. Average
4. Slightly above average
5. Above average
6. Far above average

During the LAST FOUR WEEKS, how many times have you skipped a class?

_____ times

Which of the following best describes your average grade this school year?
1. A (93-100)
2. A- (90-92)
3. B+ (87-89)
4. B (83-86)
5. B- (80-82)
6. C+ (77-79)
7. C (73-76)
8. C- (70-72)
9. D (69 or below)

On average during the school year, about how many hours per week do you work in a job? (If you don't work at all, write in a 0)

_____ hours per week

During a typical week, about how many evenings do you go out for fun and recreation? (If you don't go out at all, write in a 0)

_____ evenings per week

Following are some questions about how you view school. (Circle your answer)

Going to school has been an enjoyable experience for me.
1. Strongly agree
2. Agree somewhat
3. Disagree somewhat
4. Strongly disagree

Doing well in school is important for getting a good job.
1. Strongly agree
2. Agree somewhat
3. Disagree somewhat
4. Strongly disagree

Some people like school very much. Others don't. How do you feel about going to school?

1. I like school very much.
2. I like school quite a bit.
3. I like school some.
4. I don't like school very much.
5. I don't like school at all.

How often do you feel the schoolwork you are assigned is meaningful and important?

1. Almost always
2. Often or a lot
3. Sometimes
4. Seldom
5. Never

How interesting are most of your courses to you?

1. Very exciting and stimulating
2. Quite interesting
3. Fairly interesting
4. Slightly dull
5. Very dull

How important do you think the things you are learning in school are going to be for your later life?

1. Very important
2. Quite important
3. Fairly important
4. Slightly important
5. Not at all important

About how many time this school year have you been to see a school counselor?

_____ times this year

How helpful have your sessions with a counselor been to you?

1. Extremely helpful
2. Quite helpful
3. Somewhat helpful
4. A little helpful
5. Not at all helpful
9. Did not see a counselor this year

For the next group of questions, read each one, decide how you feel about it, and then circle either TRUE (T) or FALSE (F). If you agree with a statement, or feel that it is true about you, answer TRUE. If you disagree with a statement, or feel it is not true about you, answer FALSE. **Be sure to answer TRUE or FALSE for every statement, even if you have to guess at some.**

T F A person needs to "show off" a little now and then.

T F I have had very peculiar and strange experiences.

T F I am often said to be hotheaded.

T F I sometimes pretend to know more than I really do.

T F Sometimes I feel like smashing things.

T F Most people would tell a lie if they could gain by it.

T F I think I would enjoy having authority over other people.

T F I have sometimes stayed away from another person because I feared doing or saying something that I might regret afterwards.

T F Sometimes I feel like swearing.

T F I like to boast about my achievements now and then.

T F I must admit I often try to get my own may regardless of what others may want.

T F I would do almost anything on a dare.

T F I like to be the center of attention.

T F At times I feel like picking a fistfight with someone.

T F I do not always tell the truth.

T F I would like to wear expensive clothes.

T F I consider a matter from every standpoint before I make a decision.

T F My way of doing things is apt to be misunderstood by others.

T F Sometimes I feel as if I must injure either myself or someone else.

T F I often do whatever makes me feel cheerful here and now, even at the cost of some distant goal.

T F I can remember "playing sick" to get out of something.

T F I think I would like to fight in a boxing match sometimes.

T F I like to go to parties and other affairs where there is lots of loud fun.

T F I keep out of trouble at all costs.

T F I am apt to show off in some way if I get the chance.

| T | F | I am often bothered by useless thoughts which keep running through my mind. |

T F I am often bothered by useless thoughts which keep running through my mind.

T F I must admit that I have a bad temper, once I get angry.

T F I like large, noisy parties.

T F I am a better talker than a listener.

T F Sometimes I rather enjoy going against the rules and doing things I'm not supposed to do.

T F I have very few quarrels with members of my family.

T F I have never done anything dangerous for the thrill of it.

T F I feel that I have often been punished without cause.

T F I would like to be an actor on the stage or in movies.

T F At times I have a strong urge to do something harmful or shocking.

T F My home life was always happy.

T F I often act on the spur of the moment without stopping to think.

For the next few items choose one of the four answer to tell how you feel about the statement. Circle the number that best expresses your position.

1. strongly agree
2. agree somewhat
3. disagree somewhat
4. strongly agree

1 2 3 4 Generally, when I was younger my parents or guardians kept a pretty close eye on me.

1 2 3 4 Generally, when I was younger my parents or guardians recognized when I had done something wrong.

1 2 3 4 Generally, when I was younger my parents or guardians punished me when they knew I had done something wrong.

This section deals with behaviors that may be against the rules or against the law, and why you may have done them. We hope you will answer all of these questions. However, if you find a question you cannot answer honestly, we would prefer that you leave it blank. Remember, your answers will never be connected with your name or class.

Looking over **this past year, first** think of about how many times you did these things, and then think of the **main reason why you last did them**. If some other reason besides those listed was the main reason, describe it in just a few words.

The main reason you did it
1. I was mad, angry, frustrated
2. for fun, thrills, excitement
3. because my friends were doing it too
4. to see if I could get away with it
5. other reason (briefly explain)

About how many times This past year (if not at all, write in a 0)		**Main reason** (Circle one)
____ times	Hit an instructor or supervisor	1 2 3 4 5_____
____ times	Gotten into a serious fight at work or school	1 2 3 4 5_____
____ times	Taken part in a fight where a group group of your friends were against another group	1 2 3 4 5_____
____ times	Hurt someone badly enough to need bandages or a doctor	1 2 3 4 5_____
____ times	Used a gun or knife or some other thing (like a club) to	1 2 3 4 5_____
____ times	Taken/stolen something from someone else worth less than $50	1 2 3 4 5_____

Looking over **this past year, first** think of about how many times you did these things, and think of the **main reason why you last did them**. If some other reason besides those listed was the main reason, describe it in just a few words.

The main reason you did it
1. I was mad, angry, frustrated
2. for fun, thrills, excitement
3. because my friends were doing it too
4. to see if I could get away with it
5. other reason (briefly explain)

About how many times		**Main reason**			
This past year (if not at all, write in a 0)		(Circle one)			
____ times	Taken/stolen something from someone else worth more than $50 (example, a bicycle, a stereo, or something equally valuable)	1	2	3	4
		5_____			
____ times	Taken something from a store without paying for it (shoplifted)	1	2	3	4
		5_____			
____ times	Taken a car without permission for a "joyride"	1	2	3	4
		5_____			
____ times	Taken something from a car (tapedeck, wallet, purse, hubcaps, mirrors, etc.)without permission	1	2	3	4
		5_____			
____ times	Damaged (scratched, dented, painted, vandalized, etc.) a car on purpose	1	2	3	4
		5_____			
____ times	Gone into or broken into some house or building when you weren't supposed to be there	1	2	3	4
		5_____			

Looking over **this past year, first** think of about how many times you did these things, and then think of the **main reason why you last did them.** If some other reason besides those listed was the main reason, describe it in just a few words.

> **The main reason you did it**
> 1. I was mad, angry, frustrated
> 2. for fun, thrills, excitement
> 3. because my friends were doing it too
> 4. to see if I could get away with it
> 5. other reason   (briefly explain)

About how many times		**Main reason**			
This past year (if not at all, write in a 0)		(Circle one)			
____ times	Set fire to someone else's stuff/ property	1	2	3	4
		5_____			
____ times	Damaged school property on purpose	1	2	3	4
		5_____			
____ times	Damage property at work on purpose	1	2	3	4
		5_____			
____ times	Gotten into trouble with the police because of something you did	1	2	3	4
		5_____			

For the next few items choose one of the four answers to tell how you feel about the statement. Circle the number that best expresses your position.

1. strongly agree
2. agree somewhat
3. disagree somewhat
4. strongly disagree

1 2 3 4   I often act on the spur of the moment without stopping to think.

1 2 3 4   I don't devote much though and effort to preparing for the future.

1 2 3 4   I often do whatever brings me pleasure here and now, even at the cost of some distant goal.

1 2 3 4   I'm more concerned with what happens to me in the short run than in the long run.

1 2 3 4   I much prefer doing things that pay off right away rather than in the future.

1 2 3 4   When I have a little extra money, I'm more likely to spend it on something I really don't need than to save it for the future.

1 2 3 4   I frequently try to avoid projects that I know will be difficult.

1 2 3 4   When things get complicated, I tend to quit and withdraw.

1 2 3 4   The things in life that are easiest to do bring me the most pleasure.

1 2 3 4   I dislike really hard tasks that stretch my abilities to the limit.

1 2 3 4   I like to test myself every now and then by doing something a little risky.

1 2 3 4   Sometimes I will take a risk just for the fun of it.

1 2 3 4   I sometimes find it exciting to do things for which I might get in trouble.

1 2 3 4   Excitement and adventure are more important to me than peace and security.

1 2 3 4   If I had a choice, I would almost always rather do something physical rather than something mental.

1 2 3 4   I almost always feel better when I am on the move rather than sitting and thinking.

1. strongly agree
2. agree somewhat
3. disagree somewhat
4. strongly disagree

1 2 3 4   I like to get out and do things more than I like to read or think about things.

1 2 3 4   I seem to have more energy and a greater need for activity than most other people my age.

1 2 3 4   I try to look out for myself first, even if it means making things difficult for other people.

1 2 3 4   I'm not very sympathetic to other people when they are having problems.

1 2 3 4   If things upset other people, it's their problem not mine.

1 2 3 4   I will try to get the things I want even when I know it's causing problems for other people.

1 2 3 4   I lose my temper pretty easily.

1 2 3 4   Often when I'm angry at people I feel more like hurting them than talking to them about why I am angry.

1 2 3 4   When I am really angry other people better stay away from me.

1 2 3 4   When I have a serious disagreement with someone, it's usually hard for me to talk calmly about it without getting upset.

The next few items concern some of your habits. Just answer yes or no to the following items. (Circle the number)

1. yes
2. no

1 2   Do you use tobacco products?

1 2   Do you usually drink more than two or three alcoholic beverages during the week?

1 2   When you have a cold or some other minor sickness, do you usually take some kind of medication.

1 2   Do you pretty much eat what you feel like eating without being concerned with how it affects your health?

1 2   When you are in a car/truck, do you always use the seat belt?

1 2   Do you ever gamble or bet on anything?

1. yes
2. no

1. strongly agree
2. agree somewhat
3. disagree somewhat
4. strongly disagree

1 2   Do you sometimes spend more than you have so you end up owing money?

1 2   During the past year, have you been in an accident or injured yourself so severely that you had to see a doctor?

1 2   Do you usually wait to the last minute to do your homework?

For the next few items choose one of the four answers to tell how you feel about the statement. Circle the number that best expresses your position.

1 2 3 4   I get a real kick out of doing things that are a little dangerous.

1 2 3 4   I like to test myself every now and then by doing something a little risky.

1 2 3 4   I hardly ever crave excitement.

1 2 3 4   Sometimes I will take a risk just for the fun of it.

1 2 3 4   I have never done anything dangerous for the thrill of it.

1 2 3 4   Sometimes I rather enjoy going against the rules and doing things I'm not supposed to do.

About how many days in the past four weeks did you do each of the following? (Write in how many days you did each activity, if not at all write in a 0)

_____ days I went to the movies

_____ days I rode around in a car/truck/motorcycle just for fun

_____ days I participated in community affairs or volunteer work

_____ days I played a musical instrument or sing

_____ days I did creative writing

_____ days I actively participated in sports, athletics, or exercising

_____ days I did art or craft work

_____ days I worked around the house, yard, garden, car, etc.

_____ days I went shopping or window-shopping

_____ days I read books, magazines, or newspaper

The next few questions deal with the use of drugs and alcohol and why you may used them. We hope you can answer all the questions, but if you find one you cannot answer honestly, we would prefer that you leave it blank. Remember, your answers will never be connected with you name or class.

Looking over **the past four weeks**, first think of how many days you did these things, then think of the **one main reason why you last did them**. Circle the one answer that seems the most accurate. If some other reason besides those listed was the main reason, describe it in just a few words.

The main reason you did it
1. for fun, thrills, excitement
2. my friends were doing it too
3. it made me feel good
4. to see if I could get away wit it
5. other reasons (briefly explain)

About how many days in the past		**Main reason**
four weeks did you . . . . (if never, write in a 0)		(Circle one)
_____ days	Smoke cigarettes or chew tobacco	1 2 3 4 5 _____
_____ days	Drink beer, wine, or liquor	1 2 3 4 5 _____
_____ days	Get drunk on beer, wine, or liquor	1 2 3 4 5 _____
_____ days	Smoke marijuana, pot, hash	1 2 3 4 5 _____
_____ days	Use drugs like cocaine, crack speed, downers, heroin, LSD, or angel Dust (PCP)	1 2 3 4 5 _____

For the next group of questions, read each one, decide how you feel about it, and then circle either TRUE (T) or FALSE (F). If you agree with a statement, or feel that it is true about you, answer TRUE. If you disagree with a statement, or feel it is not true about you, answer FALSE. **Be sure to answer True or False for every statement, even if you have to guess at some.**

T F   When I was going to school Ii played hooky quite often.

T F   I think Lincoln was greater than Washington.

T F   I would do almost anything on a dare.

T F   With things going as they are, it's pretty hard to keep up hope of amounting to something.

T F   I think I am stricter about right and wrong than most people.

T F   I am somewhat afraid of the dark.

T F   My parents have often disapproved of my friends.

T F   My parents have generally let me make my own decisions.

T F   I would rather go without something than ask for a favor.

T F   I have had more than my share of things to worry about.

T F   When I meet a stranger I often think that he/she is better than I am.

T F   Before I do something I try to consider how my friends will react to it.

T F   I have never been in trouble with the law.

T F   In school I was sometimes sent to the principal because I had misbehaved.

T F   Most of the time I feel happy.

T F   I often feel as though I have done something wrong or wicked.

T F   I have often gone against my parents' wishes.

T F   I often think about how I look and what impression I am making upon others.

T F   I have never done any heavy drinking.

T F   I find it easy to "drop" or "break with" a friend.

T F   I get nervous when I have to ask someone for a job.

T F   Sometimes I used to feel that I would like to leave home.

T F   I never worry about my looks.

T F   My home life was always very pleasant.

T F   I seem to do things that I regret more often than other people do.

T F   My table manners are no quite as good at home as when I am out.

T F   It is pretty easy for people to win arguments with me.

T F   I know who is responsible for most of my troubles.

T F   I get pretty discouraged with the law when a smart lawyer gets a criminal free.

T F   I have used alcohol excessively.

T F   I sometimes wanted to run away from home.

T F   Life usually hands me a pretty raw deal.

T F   People often talk about me behind my back.

T F   I would never play cards (poker) with a stranger.

T F   I don't think I'm quite as happy as others seems to be.

T F   I used to steal sometimes when I was a youngster.

T F   My home as a child was less peaceful and quiet than those of most other people.

T F   As a child in school I used to give the teachers a lots of trouble.

T F   If the pay was right I would like to travel with a circus or carnival.

T F   I never cared much for school.

T F   The members of my family were always very close to each other.

T F   My parents never really understood me.

T F   A person is better off not to trust anyone.

You're finished!   Take a minute to look over the survey and make sure you answered all the questions. Thanks again for your help.

Bibliography

Akers, Ronald L. 2000. *Criminological Theories.* California:
Roxbury Publishing Co.

Anderson, Elijah. 1994."The Code of the Streets." *The Atlantic Monthly* May: 81-94.

Arneklev, Bruce, Harold G. Grasmick, Charles R. Tittle, and Robert J. Bursik, Jr. 1993. "Low Self-Control and Imprudent Behavior." *Journal of Quantitative Criminology* 9:225-47.

Beauvais, Frederick. 1992. "Trends in Drug Use Among American Indian Students and Dropouts, 1975-1994." *American Journal of Public Health* 86(11):1594-1598.

Beauvais, Frederick, E.R. Oetting, and W. Wolf. 1989. "American Indian Youth and Drugs, 1976-1987: A Continuing Problem." *American Journal of Public Health* 79:634-636.

Benson, Michael L. and Elizabeth Moore. 1992. "Are White Collar and Common Offenders the Same? An Empirical and Theoretical Critique of a Recently Proposed General Theory of Crime." *Journal of Research in Crime and Delinquency* 29:251-272.

Bishop, Donna M. and Charles E. Frazier. 1996. "Race Effects in Juvenile Justice Decision-Making: Findings of a Statewide Analysis." *Journal of Criminal Law and Criminology* 86:(2)392-413.

Blau, Judith, R. and Peter M. Blau. 1982. "The Cost of Inequality: Metropolitan Structure and Violent Crime." *American Sociological Review* 47:114-129.

Blumstein, Alfred, Jacqueline Cohen, Jeffery Roth, and Christy Visher. 1986. *Criminal Careers and "Career" Criminals.* Washington, D.C.: National Academy Press.

Brezina, Timothy. 1996. "Adapting to Strain: An Examination of Delinquent Coping Responses." *Criminology* 34:39-60.

Brezina, Timothy. 2000. "Delinquent Problem-Solving: An Interpretive Framework for Criminological Theory and Research." *Journal of Research in Crime and Delinquency* 37:3-31.

Center for the Study of Crime, Delinquency, and Social Control. 1994. *High School Delinquency Survey, 1991-1994.* Norman, Oklahoma: Department of Sociology, University of Oklahoma.

Cloward, Richard and Lloyd Ohlin.1960.*Delinquency and Opportunity.* New York: The Free Press.

Cochran, John K., Peter B. Wood, Christine S. Sellers, Wendy Wilkerson and Mitchell B. Chamlin. 1998. "Academic Dishonesty and Low Self-Control: An Empirical Test of a General Theory of Crime." *Deviant Behavior* 19:227-255.

Coleman, Adrian. 1994. "Self-Esteem vs Delinquency." *Youth Studies* 13(3):5-7.

Cose, Ellis. 1993. *The Rage of a Privileged Class.* New York: Harper Collins.

Cross, William E., Jr. 1991. *Shades of Black: Diversity in African-American Identity.* Philadelphia. Temple University Press.

Dweck, Carol S. 1999. *Self-Theories: Their Role in Motivation, Personality, and Development.* Philadelphia: Psychology Press.

Ellison, Christopher G. 1993. "Religious Involvement and Self-Perception Among Black Americans." *Social Forces* 71:1027-1055.

Evans, T. David, Francis T. Cullen, Velmer S. Burton, Jr., R. Gregory Dunaway, and Michael L. Benson.1997."The Social Consequences of Self-Control: Testing the General Theory of Crime." *Criminology* 35:475-501.

Glueck, Sheldon and Eleanor Glueck. 1950. *Unraveling Juvenile Delinquency*. Cambridge, Mass.: Harvard University Press.

Gold, Martin. 1978. "Scholastic Experiences, Self-Esteem, and Delinquent Behavior: A Theory for Alternative Schools." *Crime and Delinquency* 290-308.

Golden, Reid M., and Steven F. Messner. 1987. "Dimensions of Racial Inequality and Rates of Violent Crime." *Criminology* 25:525-541.

Gottfredson, Michael R. and Travis Hirschi. 1990. *A General Theory of Crime*. California: Stanford University Press.

Grasmick, Harold G., Charles R. Tittle, Robert J. Bursik, Jr., and Bruce J. Arneklev. 1993. "Testing the Core Empirical Implications of Gottfredson and Hirschi's General Theory of Crime." *Journal of Research in Crime and Delinquency* 30:5-29.

Green, Samuel B., and Neil Salkind. 2003. *Using SPSS for Windows and Macintosh*. New Jersey: Pearson Education, Inc.

Hawkins, Darnell, John H. Laub, Janet L. Lauritsen, and Lynn Cothern. 2000. "Race, Ethnicity, and Serious and Violent Juvenile Offending." *Juvenile Justice Bulletin*. Office of Juvenile Justice and Delinquency Prevention June.

Hay, Carter. 2001. "Parenting, Self-Control, and Delinquency: A Test of Self-Control Theory." *American Journal of Criminology* 39(3):707-736.

Hill, Mark. 2000. "Color Differences in the Socioeconomic Status of African American Men: Results of a Longitudinal Study." *Social Forces* 78(4):1437-1460.

Hirschi, Travis, and H. Selvin.1967. *Delinquency Research*. New York: The Free Press.

Hirschi, Travis, 1969. *Causes of Delinquency*. Berkeley: University of California Press.

Hirschi, Travis. 1976. "A Control Theory of Delinquency." Pp. 250-267 in Traub and Little (eds.), *Theories of Deviance*. Itasca: F.E. Peacock Publishers, Inc.

Hoelter, Jon W. 1983. "Factorial Invariance and Self-Esteem: Reassessing Race and Sex Differences." *Social Forces* 61(3):834-846.

Hughes, Michael and Bradley R. Hertel. 1990. "The Significance of Color Remains: A Study of Life Chances, Mate Selection, and Ethnic Consciousness among Black Americans." *Social Forces* 68(4):1105-1120.

Hughes, Michael and Melvin Thomas. (1998). "The Continuing Significance of Race Revisited: A Study of Race, Class, and Quality of Life in America, 1972 to 1996." *American Sociological Review* 63(6):785-795.

Jang, Sung Joon and Terence P. Thornberry. 1998. "Self-Esteem, Delinquent Peers, and Delinquency: A Test of the Self-Enhancement Thesis." *American Sociological Review* 585-598.

Kaplan, Diane S., and Mitchell B. Peck. 1994. "Structural Relations Model of Self-Rejection, Disposition to Deviance, and Academic Failure." *Journal of Educational Research* 87(3):166-174.

Kaplan, Howard B. 1976. "Self-Attitudes and Deviant Response." *Social Forces* 54(4):788-801.

Kaplan, Howard B.1978. "Deviant Behavior and Self-Enhancement in Adolescence." *Journal of Youth and Adolescence* 7:253-77.

Kaplan, Howard B. 1982. "Self-Attitudes and Deviant Behavior." *Youth and Society* 14(2):185-211.

Kaplan, Howard B., S. Martin, and R. Johnson. 1986. "Self-Rejection and the Explanation of Deviance: Specification of the Structure among Latent Constructs." *American Journal of Sociology* 92(2): 384-411.

Katz, Jennifer, Thomas Joiner, Jr., and Paul Kwon. 2002. "Membership in a Devalued Social Group and Emotional Well-Being: Developing a Model of Personal Self-Esteem, Collective Self-Esteem, and Group Socialization." *Sex Roles: A Journal of Research* 47(9-10):419-431.

Loeber, Rolf, and Magda Stouthamer-Loeber. 1986. "Family Factors as Correlates and Predictors of Juvenile Conduct Problems and Delinquency." In *Crime and Justice: An Annual Review of Research*, edited by M.Tonry and N. Morris. Chicago: University of Chicago Press.

Longshore, Douglas, Eunice Chang, Shih-chao Hsieh and Nena Messina. (2004). "Self-Control and Social Bonds: A Combined Control Perspective on Deviance." *Crime and Delinquency* 50(4): 542-564.

Longshore, Douglas, Susan Turner, and Judith Stein. 1996. "Self-Control in a Criminal Sample: An Examination of Construct Validity." *Criminology* 3:209-28.

Luhtanen, R., and J. Crocker. 1992. "A Collective Self-Esteem Scale: Self-Evaluation of One's Social Identity." *Personality and Social Psychology Bulletin* 18:302-318.

McCarthy, John and D. Hoge.1984. "The Dynamics of Self-Esteem and Delinquency." *American Journal of Sociology* 90(2): 396-409.

McCord, Joan.1991. "Family Relationships, Juvenile Delinquency, and Adult Criminality." *Criminology* 29: 397-417.

McKinney, Kay. 2003. "OJJDP's Tribal Youth Initiatives." *Juvenile Justice Bulletin* Office of Juvenile Justice and Delinquent Prevention.

Merton, Robert. 1938. "Social Structure and 'Anomie." *American Sociological Review* 3:672-682.

Messner, Steven F., Lawrence E. Raffalovich and Richard McMillan. 2001. "Economic Deprivation and Changes in Homicide Arrest Rates for White and Black Youths." *Criminology* 39:591-613.

Messner, Steven F. and Richard Rosenfeld. 2001. *Crime and the American Dream.* Belmont, CA.: Wadsworth.

Morenoff, Jeffrey D., Robert J. Sampson and Steven W. Raudenbush. 2001. "Neighborhood Inequality, Collective Efficacy, and the Spatial Dynamics of Urban Violence." *Criminology* 39:517-559.

Nagin, Daniel and David Farrington. 1992. "The Stability of Criminal Potential from Childhood to Adulthood." *Criminology* 30:235-260.

Nye, Ivan F. 1958. *Family Relationships and Delinquent Behavior.* New York: Wiley and Sons.

Office of Juvenile Justice Delinquency Prevention. 2003. *Child Delinquency Bulletin* "Child Delinquency: Early Intervention and Prevention." Rockville, MD.: Juvenile Justice Clearinghouse.

Office of Juvenile Justice Delinquency Prevention. 2002. *OJJDP Annual Report 2002.* Rockville, MD.: Juvenile Justice Clearinghouse.

Owens, Timothy J. 1994. "Two Dimensions of Self-Esteem: Reciprocal Effects of Positive Self-Worth and Self-Deprecation on Adolescent Problems." *American Sociological Review* 59:391-407.

Paternoster, Raymond, and Paul Mazerolle. 1994. "General Strain Theory and Delinquency: A Replication and Extension." *Journal of Research on Crime and Delinquency* 31:235-263.

Patterson, Gerald R., B.D. De Baryshe, and E. Ramsey. 1989. "A Developmental Perspective on Antisocial Behavior." *American Psychologist* 44:329-335.

Pettit, Becky and Bruce Western. 2004. "Mass Imprisonment and the Life Course: Race and Class Inequality in U.S. Incarceration." *American Sociology Review* 69: 151-169.

Porter, Judith R. and Robert E. Washington. 1979. "Black Identity and Self-Esteem: A Review of Studies of Black Self-Concept." *Annual Review of Sociology* 5:53-74.

Pratt, Travis C., and Francis Cullen. 2000. "The Empirical Status of Gottfredson and Hirschi's General Theory of Crime: A Meta-analysis." *Criminology* 38:931-964.

Reckless, Walter. 1961. "A Non-Causal Explanation: Containment Theory." In *Theories of Deviance*, edited by Stuart H. Traub and Craig B. Little. Pp. 306-312. Itasca: F.E. Peacock Publishers, Inc.

Reckless, Walter and Simon Dinitz. 1967. "Pioneering with Self-Concept as a Vulnerability Factor in Delinquency." *The Journal of Criminal Law, Criminology and Police Science* 58(4):515-523.

Reiss, Albert J., Jr. 1950. "Delinquency as the Failure of Personal and Social Controls." *American Sociological Review* 16:196-207.

Richter, Linda and Patrick Johnson. 2001. "Current Methods of Assessing Substance Use: A Review of Strengths, Problems, and Developments." *Journal of Drug Issues* 31(4):809-832.

Rosenberg, Morris, Carmi Schooler, and Carrie Schoenbach. 1989. "Self-Esteem and Adolescent Problems: Modeling Reciprocal Effects." *American Sociological Review* 54:1004-1017.

Ross, Lee E. 1994. "The Impact of Race-Esteem and Self-Esteem on Delinquency." *Sociological Focus* 27(2):111-124.

Sampson, Robert J. 1985. "Race and Criminal Violence: A Demographically Disaggregated Analysis of Urban Homicide." *Crime and Delinquency* 31:47-82.

Sampson, Robert J. and John H. Laub. 1993. "Structural Variations in Juvenile Court Processing: Inequality, the Underclass, and Social Control." *Law & Society Review* 27: 2.

Sampson, Robert J. and Janet L. Lauritsen. 1997. "Racial and Ethnic Disparities in Crime and Criminal Justice in the United States." *Crime and Justice* 21:311-374.

Shoemaker, Donald. 2000. *Theories of Delinquency.* New York: Oxford University Press.

Snyder, Howard, and Melissa Sickmund. 1995. "Juvenile Courts and Juvenile Crime." *Juvenile Offenders and Victims: A National Report,* pp.123-137. Washington, DC: Office of Juvenile Justice and Delinquency Prevention.

Snyder, Howard. 2001. "Epidemiology of Official Offending." In *Child Delinquents: Development, Intervention, and Service Needs,* edited by R. Loeber and D.P. Farrington. Thousand Oaks, CA: Sage Publications, Inc.

Snyder, Howard N. 2004. *Juvenile Justice Bulletin.* "Juvenile Arrests 2002." Washington, D.C.: U.S. Government Printing Office.

Tittle, Charles. 2000. "Theoretical Developments in Criminology." In *The Nature of Crime: Continuity and Change* 1:51-101. Washington, DC: U.S. Department of Justice, Office of Justice Programs.

United States Department of Education. 2001. *Surgeon General's Report.* Washington, D.C.: U.S. Government Printing Office.

Vazsonyi, Alexander T., Lloyd Pickering, Marianne Junger and Dick Hessing. 2001. "An Empirical Test of a General Theory of Crime: A Four Nation Comparative Study of Self-Control and the Prediction of Deviance." *Journal of Research in Crime and Delinquency* 38(2):91-132.

Wells, Edward L. 1989. "Self-Enhancement Through Delinquency: A Conditional Test of Self-Derogation Theory." *Journal of Research in Crime and Delinquency* 26(3):226-252.

Wells, Edward L. and J. Rankin. 1983. "Self-Concept as a Mediating Factor in Delinquency." *Social Psychology Quarterly* 46(1):11-22.

West, Donald, and David Farrington. 1973. *Who Becomes Delinquent?* London: Heinemann.

Wolfgang, Marvin and Franco Ferracuti. 1967. *The Subculture of Violence: Towards an Integrated Theory in Criminology.* Beverly Hills, California: Sage.

Wood, Peter B., Betty Pfefferbaum, and Bruce J. Arneklev. 1993. "Risk-taking and Self-Control: Social Psychological Correlates of Delinquency. *Journal of Crime and Justice* 16:111-130.

Wood, Peter B., John K. Cochran, Betty Pfefferbaum, and Bruce J. Arneklev. 1995. "Sensation-Seeking and Delinquent Substance Use: An Extension of Leaning Theory." *Journal of Drug Issues* 25:173-193.

Wood, Peter B. and W. Charles Clay. 1996. "Perceived Structural Barriers and Academic Performance Among American Indian High School Students." *Youth and Society* 28(1): 40-60.

Wood, Peter B., Walter R. Gove, James A Wilson, and John K. ochran. 1997. "Nonsocial Reinforcement and Habitual Criminal Conduct: An Extension of Learning Theory." *Criminology* 35:355-366.

Wylie, R.C. 1978. *The Self-Concept: Theory and Research on Selected Topics Vol.2*. Revised edition. Lincoln: University of Nebraska Press.

Index

achievement, 125
African Americans, vii, viii, 2,
    10, 16, 18, 20, 21, 26, 31,
    34, 35, 36, 38, 39, 41, 42,
    44, 45, 51, 54, 58, 62, 64,
    65, 77, 79, 80, 81, 82, 83,
    85, 97, 98, 99, 101, 103,
    109, 110, 111, 117, 118,
    119, 120, 121, 122, 123,
    124, 125, 126, 127, 129, 130
age, 1, 10, 14, 15, 19, 20, 22,
    30, 31, 33, 35, 36, 37, 38,
    44, 53, 54, 56, 58, 59, 60,
    62, 64, 65, 75, 85, 88, 95,
    98, 101, 103, 111, 113, 123,
    141, 199, 209
Akers, 7, 12, 17, 123, 128, 131
Anderson, 1, 131
Arneklev, 13, 30, 43, 51, 131,
    133, 139
attachment, 1, 6, 7, 12, 15, 17,
    29, 34, 35, 36, 43, 44, 45,
    47, 51, 54, 56, 59, 60, 62,
    65, 67, 69, 73, 81, 88, 89,
    91, 93, 94, 95, 97, 98, 105,
    106, 110, 114, 117, 118,
    120, 122, 123, 125, 128
average grade, 31, 33, 35, 36,
    37, 44, 53, 54, 56, 58, 59,
    60, 62, 64, 65, 73, 77, 79,
    80, 88, 92, 93, 95, 98, 101,
    103, 124, 125, 200
Benson and Moore, 12

Bishop and Frazier, 21
Blumstein, 15, 131
bonding, 1, 2, 1, 4, 5, 6, 7, 14,
    17, 22, 23, 28, 31, 32, 33,
    34, 36, 37, 40, 43, 47, 51,
    53, 54, 58, 59, 60, 62, 64,
    65, 66, 95, 97, 101, 105,
    106, 113, 114, 115, 116,
    117, 118, 119, 120, 122,
    123, 125, 128, 129, 130
Brezina, 113, 114, 125, 132
causal process, 17
Cloward and Ohlin, 16
collective identities, 11
continuum, 1, 18, 113
Cross, 10, 123, 125, 132
Delinquency, viii, ix, x, 2, 18,
    19, 20, 21, 25, 26, 27, 33,
    55, 57, 68, 69, 73, 74, 75,
    78, 79, 82, 83, 89, 90, 93,
    94, 102, 112, 131, 132, 133,
    134, 135, 136, 137, 138,
    139, 143, 145, 146, 147,
    148, 149, 150, 151, 152,
    153, 154, 155, 156, 157,
    158, 159, 160, 161, 162,
    163, 164
Dinitz, 7, 8, 137
discipline, 1, 6, 11, 12, 13, 14,
    128
ethnic differences in crime, 15,
    16
Evans, 13, 132

Printed in the United States
207831BV00001B/185/P